DEDICATION

This book is dedicated to all of the compassionate caregivers serving the Tapestries residents at United Methodist Communities. They come to work each day as a personal mission and pour their hearts and souls into providing care, support, and a normal life for those living with a dementia diagnosis.

Foreword by James Keach

Director of *Glen Campbell: I'll Be Me* and *Turning Point*

Avandell

REIMAGINING THE DEMENTIA EXPERIENCE

LARRY CARLSON

Industry Champion, Visionary & Thought Leader

Avandell: Reimagining the Dementia Experience

Published by TVGuestpert Publishing

ISBN-13: 978-1-7358981-5-5
BISAC CODES: HEA039140, FAM017000, FAM005000

Nationwide Distribution through Ingram & New Leaf Distributing Company.

TVGuestpert & TVGuestpert Publishing are visionary media companies that seek to educate, enlighten, and entertain the masses with the highest level of integrity. Our full-service production company, publishing house, management, and media development firm promise to engage you creatively and honor you and ourselves, as well as the community, in order to bring about fulfillment and abundance both personally and professionally.

Front Book Cover Design by Tanja Prokop

Book Design by Carole Allen Design Studio

Author headshot by Nader Boctor

Edited by TVGuestpert Publishing

11664 National Blvd, #345

Los Angeles, CA. 90064

310-584-1504

www.TVGuestpertPublishing.com

www.TVGuestpert.com

First Printing 2022

10 9 8 7 6 5 4 3 2 1

ACKNOWLEDGMENTS

TO MY FAMILY:

To my wife, Melanie, who, as a new bride, was willing to move into a senior community when I took my first job as a nursing home administrator. And who has always supported me in my professional journey.

To my daughters, Meredith, Marisa, and Mindy, who were willing to share themselves with many of the seniors I served over the years.

TO MY PROFESSIONAL MENTORS OVER THE YEARS:

Maurice Rolfe—Board Treasurer of a not-for-profit senior living community who took a chance and hired a twenty-three-year-old as administrator . . . my first job.

E. Drew Gackenheimer—who saw potential in me and provided the opportunity to grow in my profession.

L. Bradford Perkins—who introduced me to thoughtful design to support aging services and has been a good friend all along the journey.

Sister Frances Clare Radke—a beautiful human who inspired me and showed me how to drive mission and values into the fabric of an organization so that the culture comes alive in service to others.

Rev. Dr. Virginia Samuel Cetuk—the board chair who brought me to UMC and supported and challenged me in my role as a new CEO.

Rick Stiffney—whose thoughtful, pragmatic conversations guided me, especially deepening my strategic planning and visioning processes.

The Board of Directors of United Methodist Communities—whose support and encouragement allowed me to lead the organization into new ways to impact ministry to seniors.

TO MY NUMEROUS MANAGEMENT TEAMS OVER THE YEARS:

I've had the privilege of working with some truly amazing, smart, and dedicated individuals over my professional career. It was always an honor to lead and serve with them for the elders entrusted to our care. There have been good times and challenging times, but together we persevered in our service.

TO THE AVANDELL DEVELOPMENT TEAM:

Eloy van Hal and Janette Spiering from De Hogeweyk™—who inspired me to bring this new paradigm for dementia care to the United States.

Pam Garofolo—whose dedication to those people living with dementia inspired me in the development of the pragmatics and programming of Avandell.

Cindy Jacques—who brought the voice of service to the conversation.

Robbie Voloshin—whose creative thinking on all things marketing and communications made the Avandell brand come alive.

Bob Peterson—who tirelessly managed the budget and kept us financially on track.

Travis Gleinig—who drove the tech culture at UMC in strategic and pragmatic ways.

Sandy Brown, Esq.—Corporate Counsel for over thirty years and passionate cheerleader of all things UMC.

The Perkins Eastman Design Team: David Hoglund, Max Winters and Susan DeFlitch.

The Baker Tilly Development Team: Beverly Asper, Chris Tritsis and Spencer Skinner.

The SweetWater Construction Team: Ron Witt, Nancy Witt and Dave Johnson.

The BrandMettle Team: Amy LaGrant and Matt Brown.

The TVGuestpert Team: Jacquie Jordan, Louise Elton and Hugh Taylor.

Subject Matter Experts: David Taylor, MD, Andrew Erdman, LCSW, Susan Moen, Rabbi Jeffrey J. Sirkman, Ted Sturman, Michael Corkery, Erika Updegrove, PsyD, Jackie Petruzzelli, RN.

TO GOD . . .

Who always showed up at the most challenging of times giving me comfort through scripture. Jeremiah 29:11 *For I know the plans I have for you, declares THE LORD, plans to prosper you and not to harm you, plans to give you hope and a future.*

TABLE OF CONTENTS

FOREWORD

When I started making the documentary *Turning Point*, I didn't realize the journey it would take me on. Our film started with a five-week schedule and turned into two and a half years because the story of Alzheimer's is a severe issue that's growing and growing as generations go on. There is nothing to slow or stop it, so we must find a cure. It's something that I am so passionate about.

There is an intimacy that happens when you are not afraid to speak freely and ask questions to those with Alzheimer's, and I learned that with Glen Campbell when we were filming *I'll Be Me*. To shy away from the moments of confusion, frustration, and rage that come with Alzheimer's is dishonest. We must grow empathy for it. Most people are given a severe diagnosis and give up; Glen didn't do that. He didn't want to "hang up." He wasn't afraid. *I'll Be Me* is a film that brought people with dementia and Alzheimer's freedom from shame. The power of this story compelled people, and I felt that if it could change lives, then it was a story that needed to be told. It brought a face and humanity to those with Alzheimer's.

Statistically speaking:

- 1 out of 2 people who are over the age of 85 will have some form of dementia or Alzheimer's.
- Five and a half million people are living with dementia today in America.
- 44 million people have it worldwide.
- By the year 2025, the cost of Alzheimer's care will exceed the national defense budget.
- By the year 2050, 100 million people worldwide will have it.

What to do?

- It's a brain disease. Medicine has always struggled to keep up with new problems because we live longer. The brain is still something we do not fully understand. This is something we need to start giving serious attention to.

- We created a conversation about helping others deal with this and to lift their spirits as I have been able to do with my films.

Keep that conversation going! That's my motto! And that is exactly what Larry Carlson does here in his book, *Avandell: Reimagining the Dementia Experience*. Through his work as CEO of United Methodist Communities and inspired by De Hogeweyk™ in Holland, Larry is spearheading a new way to think about how we help our relatives with Alzheimer's by creating dementia villages that better meet their needs and by overriding the institutional model of care and housing.

This problem is not going to go away, and until we rethink our approach, we have the potential to be crushed by this disease as a society while our family members and loved ones suffer.

In *Avandell: Reimagining the Dementia Experience*, Larry takes us through the revisioning of housing step by step to application and how care, costs, love, and acceptance in the placement of family members can cross a new threshold into a different way of experiencing the Long Good-bye.

—James Keach

James Keach is a Grammy and Golden Globe–winning director, producer, and actor. His film Walk the Line earned Reese Witherspoon the Academy Award for best actress. Glen Campbell: I'll Be Me *was nominated for an Academy Award and Linda Ronstadt's Sound of My Voice won both a Grammy and a Broadcast Critics Award for Best Documentary. He is a passionate advocate for bringing awareness to the tsunami facing the world with the onslaught of Alzheimer's and being a cause for change.*

INTRODUCTION:

Eleven years ago, as the new President and CEO of United Methodist Commu nities (UMC), I began thinking there must be a better way to care for those living with dementia. I, along with the United Methodist Communities leadership team, began discussing and thinking through the whole notion of dementia care in the United States. The institutional setting, which is the current model of care, doesn't serve those living with dementia.

After serving in senior living for over forty-five years, I felt there was a better way to provide a meaningful, authentic, and engaging life for those living with dementia. I witnessed so many poorly thought through care paradigms. It was like watching lives that were once full and vibrant reduced to meaninglessness. This included, not only the person with the diagnosis, but their family and caregivers.

My first initiative as the new President & CEO at UMC was to move the care paradigm from the traditional mode of treating behaviors to treating stressors and distress in a diagnosed person's life. This was a sea change in the care paradigm. UMC branded this new paradigm, naming it Tapestries because every person's life is a tapestry of their life experience. Collectively, the UMC leadership team had seen so many who had lost their meaning in the process of living with dementia. We were determined to change that and incorporate it into the way we deliver care and create an environment in our own UMC full-service communities, which allows individuals to experience life on their own terms. We developed a learning curriculum to train our staff in the ways of Tapestries, and this was subsequently accredited by the Alzheimer's Association.

At this point, I felt it wasn't enough. While programming is ultimately important, the institutional environment needed to change to support the programming. At a UMC Board of Directors strategic planning session, the leadership and Board asked the question, "How do we take Tapestries to the next level?"

My wife Melanie and I had visited De Hogeweyk™ in Amsterdam: the first in the world village where every resident lives with a dementia diagnosis. It was truly inspirational, and I felt led to bring this concept back to the United States. Socialized medicine in the Netherlands paved the way there, but the lack of a payor source would make it a challenge in the U.S. This new care paradigm would need to be competitive with the daily rates in the U.S. dementia care system.

Once back in the States, I assembled a think tank of the best minds, consisting of a team of architects, financial consultants, and the UMC Tapestries thinkers. We held numerous visioning sessions on what we were trying to accomplish and how we might be able to advance such a challenging and important conversation. The UMC Board of Directors fully supported this endeavor, as they always felt an organizational role was to be "leaven" for the industry: to model and deliver new ways of living and care within the senior living sector. UMC became committed to making the De Hoqeweyk™ concept a reality in the U.S. and the idea of Avandell was born.

Avandell is bigger than any one person; as well it should be. This alone makes it an exciting project for any CEO. Avandell is UMC's ministry product and has the potential to change the world for the next generation of seniors and their families living with dementia. My role has been one of visionary, then translating that vision into a very detailed program document (how exactly Avandell will operate), designing the village concept and blueprints, finding an appropriate site, completing a feasibility study, and assembling a team who can deliver on the vision.

As I prepared to retire at age seventy, it was important for me to transition the execution of the Avandell vision to the next generation of UMC leadership. They are capable, inspired, and dedicated to deliver on what I feel is the most important and impactful dementia living and care paradigm change in the past thirty years. I truly believe it will change the world for the next generation of seniors living with dementia.

I feel that this book is the exclamation point on my forty-five-year career in senior living and I want to continue to champion the cause. I can hardly wait for ground-breaking and subsequent ribbon cutting on the day Avandell unveils itself to the world.

WHY IS A DEMENTIA VILLAGE NEW TO THE UNITED STATES?

The successful experiment that is De Hogeweyk™ dementia village has also been replicated in several other European countries. So far, we seem to be the first in the United States to attempt this new way of supporting people. Our being the first highlights the differences between the U.S. healthcare system and that of the Netherlands. The E.U. has socialized medicine, which makes it easier, at least in theory, to make a place like De Hogeweyk™ a reality that is accessible to all of its citizens, irrespective of ability to pay.

Having been in this industry for decades, I know that the physical facilities are not the main driver of success in the dementia care model. My peers know that building a safe village is not enough. Having a dementia care model like Tapestries already in place at UMC gives us the groundwork for success with Avandell. Staff are prepared with targeted training to help make Avandell prosper.

Few providers in our industry are this far along with creating newer and better care choices. Our goal is to establish the pattern and enable other organizations to emulate what we are doing because a comparable approach that can work in the U.S. requires an overhaul of outdated senior care.

UMC is conscious of establishing a scalable and transferrable template model for other villages to be built. Avandell won't be so unique where only UMC can successfully manage a dementia care village. We are not trying to be exclusive. We're trying to make a difference as leaders and pioneers in this new model of care in the United States.

UMC is dedicated to future generations of people who are dealing with a dementia diagnosis. We want them to receive the best care and live a much better life than they could in traditional assisted living, home care, and nursing homes.

WHAT'S INSIDE

I begin the book by introducing you to two families. One is a married couple, the Millers. The other family is the Petersons. The adult children are struggling to cope with their mother's progressive dementia.

In chapter two, we learn about the revolutionary model De Hogeweyk™ dementia village in Holland that inspired UMC to launch the Avandell program. Even after forty-five years in this field, I was totally blown away by the innovation and outside-the-box thinking I witnessed when Melanie and I visited this amazing community. It was truly inspiring. This led UMC and me to push new boundaries in dementia care through Avandell in the U.S.

Chapter three, "Lives in Transition," we see firsthand how dementia affected the Millers and the Petersons. The chapter provides an overview of dementia and discusses how the disease inevitably impacts everyone in the family as everyone transitions and evolves.

Chapter four, "Arriving at the Moment of Family Crisis," looks at how dementia almost always causes an unbearable strain on the family taking care of a loved one with dementia. They arrive at what I call "the point of impossibility," where realistically, living comfortably at home is simply unsustainable. This moment causes a cascade of difficult emotions, even in the healthiest families. They need to make decisions about care. Not easy.

Chapters five and six examine current care options, medical best practices, and what's working well in the current model. In these chapters, I explore the pros and cons of home care and various types of memory care through the work I've learned at UMC. We learn about the sorts of treatments available and some of the medical standards and governance boards that approve their use. Chapter six, "What Is Working Well in the Current Model, and What Could Be Better?" goes deeper into the heart of dementia care and sets up the fundamental question I'm trying to ask in this book: "What will it take to get better at dementia care?" and what kind of environment is best for people with dementia, so they can live as normal and stress-free lifestyle as possible?

Chapter seven, "Seeking a Solution," attempts to define what the success of an ideal dementia community will look like and achieve. As a manager, this is really the crux of the matter. It's one thing to say, "Let's improve dementia care." What counts is understanding how you're going to do it and what the end result will be.

Chapter eight introduces the full Avandell model encompassing all the information we know and have learned. It describes theories of treatment that have brought the Avandell concept to the reality of implementation. These include UMC's Tapestries™ model of memory care that seeks to weave in elements of real life with the residents' former lives, weaving both into the care environment. We explore how Avandell aims to unite the empowered self through a meaningful place and authentic community, coupled with the power of nature and a sense of home.

In Chapter nine, "Realizing the Avandell Vision," is about how we took what we learned in Holland and adapted the concept for an American care and financial model. In this chapter, we debut our pilot project to turn the Avandell vision into a physical, tangible reality with a proposed community in the United States. The chapter delves into the community's design and operations and offers a view of residents' lives, along with the impact on the family and their experience in the process.

Avandell represents an opportunity to improve dementia care across the industry. People with dementia can live lives of meaning. We want to share our ideas and achievements with our peers who manage memory care residences throughout the country. Achieving this objective includes the local community's participation and blessing, as we invite them (adults and children) to visit us, participate, and make Avandell a part of their lives.

This book does not offer an answer for every challenging question about dementia care. I doubt such a book could ever be written. However, my hope is that this book will help you become better informed about dementia and how it affects those who live with it. UMC and I provide families with information and perspective and explain how dementia is treated. Hopefully, this book will help you gain a solid understanding of the new directions in dementia care and how the Avandell model is poised to take the experience of living with dementia to a new, higher level of a well-lived life with satisfaction and joy. Ideally, you will have ideas about choices and how Avandell will enable someone with dementia to live the life they love, regardless of the level of their dementia.

The information in this book is for anyone who is involved in caring for a person with dementia. The ideas I share may also be valuable and of interest to those considering a care plan for people with dementia. It's intended for families, caregivers and fellow elder care professionals. The book by design does not go into great depth on issues of dementia care. There are many excellent resources already available for that. Instead, I offer a realistic and hopeful glimpse into the future of dementia care based on my personal experiences and of those families with whom I have worked with over the years.

—Larry Carlson

CHAPTER 1
LIVING WITH DEMENTIA

"Sorry we're late," said the well-dressed, eighty-something woman as she arrived at the office with her husband. She held his arm as they maneuvered into the conference room. The man looked confused and hesitant, taking cues from his wife, on whom he was obviously quite dependent.

"I finally found the keys," she said. "This time, they were in the freezer."

The couple took a seat at the table while I sat on the other side with the Sales Director. Today was the day I chose to observe the move-in process as CEO of United Methodist Communities (UMC). My responsibilities include observing different departments and checking in on various aspects of operations. This is how we evaluate and optimize how we do things here. The supervision is necessary, as we strictly adhere to compliance regulations for senior living communities.

The woman was flustered and looked really exhausted, which was a reminder of why one of the bestselling books on dementia care is called *The 36-Hour Day*. This very tired lady was living that reality.

I told her, "Please don't worry about being delayed at all. This sort of thing happens all the time."

Working with individuals with dementia offers an opportunity to continually bring hope, safety, and reassurance. The overriding mandate for the entire organization is to listen with respect to everyone involved. We impart dignity without being patronizing and are vigilant in realizing that every person with dementia and every situation is different. This is a core principle of ours. No interaction or person is the same as the next. On our end, the way to be prepared is to keep dignity at the forefront, knowing that one day it may be our turn, and we might be the person on the other side of the conference table.

It is important to start with the premise that "normal is no longer normal." I have heard stories about microwave dinners being put in sock drawers, so hearing about keys in the freezer is just part of what we're used to hearing. Over the past forty years of managing elder care communities, I have been privy to so many heartbreaking and sometimes traumatic family stories about a "once fine and crystal-clear mind" slipping away into oblivion.

The Millers, the couple seated across the table, were both involved in the sciences. In their professions, Judith and Thomas (her husband of fifty-two years) had significantly contributed to scientific research and many key discoveries. This was the elephant in the room—the irony of "losing" an incredibly full life, as I have seen hundreds of times. This sweet gentleman was once brilliant. He was "a force venerated by the global scientific community," as one of his peers once said. Family members were still stunned and in the "How can this be happening?" mode.

Losing such a brilliant mind and dealing with this tragedy is one of the reasons that his wife and family delayed this inevitable moment and were unable to bring themselves to put him "in the home." There had not been the celebration and reward of retirement for the golden years they could enjoy together. They negotiated with "the heavens." They didn't need the gold watch. They needed him. The despair was palpable, and the new reality that had been building was, for them, unimaginable.

Dementia is cruel. Many religions and everyday people attribute growing older to being in the hands of fate or God. When he explored losing control to fate, George Mann, in *The Executioner's Heart*, wrote, "But time is a cruel mistress . . ." At UMC, however, this does not mean that we give up on our fellow man. Not at all.

There is no way to know what the future will bring. We must meet the "now." Dementia is an equal opportunity disease. Available medications to date try to slow down the rate of memory loss. There are no magic buttons (yet) from a medical technology company to reboot the brain or the personality, nor can any medications cure the myriad conditions that cause or perpetuate dementia. The scientific community affirms that promising pharmaceuticals differ from person to person because everyone has their own biochemistry and genetics combined with their past and present environmental influences. No amount of money thrown into the mix can change the ultimate outcome. At least not today.

The details and years of marriage and success were so fresh in Judith's mind, along with those of their children and colleagues. Sitting next to her, the professor could not grasp the significance of a house key. What was it for? What did it mean to lock a door? The granular things we know eluded him. There was a sense of having one's life robbed of everything good and meaningful. The grief, exhaustion, and residue of tears on the face of his stoic wife were obvious.

We then heard the familiar question we received most often from families at this stage, "Now what do we do?"

Our Sales Director started to explain options and solutions we could provide the family if they wanted to work with UMC. We offer a number of residential program choices, all of which are excellent for medical standards of care.

Judith listened intently. She did not have it in her anymore to keep up with the 24/7 care of her husband without risking her own physical and mental health. Her children lived in three different states, and none of them could leave their own families and careers. Managing everything was taking a terrible toll, and the family was finally able to talk her into exploring UMC.

EXPLORING THE IDEA OF DOING THINGS DIFFERENTLY

While I am immensely proud of what we have been able to achieve at UMC, I have also been inspired to see that there is room to do things differently and perhaps even better. Inspiration came from visiting and learning about dedicated memory care "villages" specifically designed around the needs and care of people with various levels of dementia and Alzheimer's disease.

UMC and I are taking a new approach to dementia care. This is where the Avandell paradigm comes in. Based on some fascinating breakthroughs in the design and function of treatment facilities and care originating in the Netherlands and other areas of Europe, Avandell is building a unique, dedicated environment for residents in a new dementia care community. **The ethos of Avandell is to honor the life of a person with dementia, keep them safe, and provide a normal environment.**

The Avandell dementia village brings guidance, sensitivity, and practical, targeted support to residents, families, and caregivers. The purpose of this new approach in memory care is to enable the resident to experience life and love in spite of a dementia diagnosis. According to one of our spiritual friends, Rabbi Jeffrey Sirkman, we "meet them where they are." The goal is to make it possible and seamless for people to live the lives they love, regardless of the level of their dementia.

A NEW TAKE ON THE INSTITUTIONAL MODEL OF DEMENTIA CARE

UMC and its vision have grown like a "phoenix." There is a treatment departure from the original "institutional model" of memory care. Elevating standards of care has become a necessity. People live longer. Medicine has seen to that. However, living longer means more and different diseases that come with old age.

My vision, and the vision of UMC, is a departure from previous care models. From an industry perspective, we are evolving toward different ways people can live in comfort. They should feel that their surroundings are familiar, with fewer rooms and more support staff per person, as opposed to being placed in a unit based on needs and the ability to interact. In the past, facilities and aged care corporations "put residents in their little area," which is a benign version of "being put away." It is unfortunate not to have normal, daily interactions with a person's preferred community and activities.

Facilities for the elderly usually consist of twelve to twenty-five or even forty rooms with at least one central area for residents. People have their own small room and sit down for dinner in one or two sittings. The facility manages the nursing staff and a full roster of caregivers, or "aides." Management monitors activities, food service, housekeeping, worship, and all parts of daily living.

In contrast, you've got the in-home model. This features home health visits or supervision from family caregivers so the client can stay in their current environment.

Avandell sets itself apart by putting "home" within the village. At Avandell, there will be fifteen cottages or "homes" that will house seven people with dementia.

Avandell fuses the best of home care with the efficiency and professionalism of a dementia care community. It offers an integrated village, again, "taking your community and shrinking it down a little bit." Residents have professional elder care supervision, but at Avandell, their lives will not be controlled.

One of Avandell's strong beliefs is that people with dementia should participate and have a sense of purpose in their own lives. There is life, and then there is living, so we are trying to give them a happy and dignified life even though they're living with this condition.

HOW DID I GET HERE?

To understand how I got to this point, it makes sense to go way back to when I graduated from college with no credentials for caring for seniors. I had an interest in health care and decided it would be a logical career path. This led to earning my nursing home license credentials in 1975. If you do the math, you're right. I've been doing this since the disco era. The Chicago Cubs were sixty-seven years into their 108-year losing streak in the World Series. That long.

I'd just gotten married. My first job was at a not-for-profit, community-based thirty-nine-bed facility in the Boston area. These used to be called rest homes; now, we know them as various versions of assisted living. One of the requirements for that job was that you had to live in the facility. You have to realize that I was just twenty-three at the time, and my staff affectionately called me the "boy administrator." My amazing wife of only one year and I actually moved into that nursing home together for my first job, and that was my initial exposure to senior living.

In that role as facility administrator, I was solely responsible for supervision of food service, facility maintenance, activities, nursing, and management of essential office staff. A downside of an evening could be when the night shift called out. I'd get a call on my intercom saying, "Mr. Carlson, the nurse called from the gas station with a flat tire and is going to be late tonight." And I would think, *I'm not a nurse*, but I had to deal with it.

We were there for five years. Our families and friends thought we were crazy, yet our marriage grew stronger from the experience. One of our small pleasures was, given that my wife was working at the local hospital as Chief Medical Technologist of the laboratory, when she came home from work, dinner was always brought up by our wonderful kitchen staff.

Fast forward. I'm still married to the same woman. We'll be celebrating our forty-eighth wedding anniversary next summer. This is amazing because I used to think that only "old people" would be married that long. WOW.

My next job brought me to the Rehabilitation Center for the Aging in Boston as Director of Housing, followed by a four-year stint as Assistant Executive Director at what is now called Morse Senior Life in West Palm Beach Florida. I helped build their expansion project. Then we relocated to Chicago, stayed for twenty years and raised our beautiful daughters.

In Chicago, I worked for two very caring not-for-profit, faith-based organizations—the United Church of Christ and then Franciscan Communities, where I was Senior Vice President of Operations. These fantastic experiences in senior care set the stage for me to be considered as the CEO of United Methodist Communities, which I accepted in 2011.

AN EVOLVING INDUSTRY

The industry has changed a great deal during these decades. There have been many highs and lows. Regulations, medicine, compliance, and standards of care are now more stringent. The progress made in care has been fantastic.

By far, there are many, many good and dedicated people who work in the elder care industry. We shake when colleagues in the industry are charged with elder abuse, fraud, and everything else that comes with bad publicity from bad people. I call them the few "bad apples." These negative events should not paint a distorted picture for the entire industry. Instead, these moments become turning points for the public, and then unfortunately regulations and oversight to protect seniors are put into place.

I can tell you that these rude awakenings reinforced my resolve to provide our residents with the kindest and most aware care to keep them safe. Now, as before, there are so many wonderful places where seniors live. There certainly are quality-focused facilities across the United States. The overall trend, though, has been reaching for a better standard of care. Folks who used to be in hospitals now live in nursing homes. People who used to be in a nursing home are now living in assisted living. And people who were in assisted living are now living in independent living or a version of dedicated home care. The evolution of what is now being offered targets a person's needs and transitions them into more advanced care only when needed.

Many extra services have been made available to seniors. These levels of care are more efficient and cost-effective. We have a better understanding of the aging process and have implemented so many programs that bring joy and fulfillment to our residents.

Unfortunately, in the past, restraints were used. People who were determined to be a danger to themselves or "out of control" were tied to wheelchairs or straight chairs with belts. The treatment had more to do with treating the behaviors and not the distress. There was also the use of psychotropic and antipsychotic medications to keep down the noise and let staff care for the entirety of a ward. Fortunately, today such practices are rare.

The knowledge base, especially around dementia care, has dramatically improved over the last thirty years. The last several years have seen tremendous sharing of information among those of us working in aged care. For example, when I was working at the West Palm Beach nursing facility, we had a third floor unit where folks who had memory and cognitive disorders all lived together. The way things used to be were sad for the residents and for those who would visit. We have more information now and optimal methods of making people comfortable.

UMC AND SENIOR LIVING

I feel very fortunate to be associated with UMC, an organization with a long history of innovation. Indeed, I am not sure if a concept like Avandell could be tried anywhere else.

In 1907, a committee of women appointed by the New Brunswick Preachers corresponded with pastors and members of the Methodist Episcopal churches of Monmouth County, New Jersey, about the importance of establishing a home for the aged. In response to this need, a single home at 63 Clark Avenue in Ocean Grove was purchased and United Methodist Communities was founded.

Over the next few decades, the organization expanded with Methodist Manor (Branchville in 1961), The Shores in Ocean City in 1963, Collingswood in 1971 and Pitman in 1974. A Continuing Care Retirement Community, Bristol Glen, opened in 2001 and expanded the UMC presence in northern New Jersey. Major renovations have occurred over the years at all the established full-service communities.

Beginning in 1982, UMC partnered with the US Department of Housing and Urban Development (HUD) and local churches to develop senior housing with Wesley by the Bay in Ocean City. Partnering with HUD and two local churches, Bishop Taylor opened in 1989 in East Orange; three more were added between 1994 and 2002: The Wesleyan in Red Bank, Covenant Place in Plainfield, and PineRidge of Montclair. In 2016, the organization launched HomeWorks, a home-care company. In 2018, UMC embarked on developing the first dementia village in the United States, Avandell.

Today, United Methodist Communities operates nine senior housing, assisted living, memory care, and skilled nursing facilities in the State of New Jersey serving 1,600 residents with over 1,000 associates. Homecare offices serve residents in their homes throughout much of the state. The home office of UMC is located in Neptune, New Jersey.

UMC's mission is dedicated to compassionately serving in community so that all are free to choose abundant life. UMC is expanding its scope of care to now include all-inclusive dementia villages. We help seniors with various levels of health who need assistance, as well as individuals rehabilitating from illness or surgery, those with disabilities, and people living with dementia. Mind, body, and spirit are respected with the best quality of life—the daily goal.

THE BIGGER PICTURE

The time has come to turn Avandell from an idea into a reality. UMC and I are pursuing this project at a time when American society is grappling with dementia as it never has before. Now is the time for new thinking on dementia care, and not a minute too soon.

Today's perception of growing older has evolved to the point where a great number of people fear dementia and Alzheimer's disease—so much so that people become paralyzed with fear and keep putting off critical decision-making. They are truly petrified to put a service plan in place. It is an ending of sorts, and we try to help them with their decision because it is sometimes traumatic for children, spouses, friends, and colleagues to see the final journey of the loved one with dementia.

Despite many impressive accomplishments, the elder care industry has not kept up with new or better ways to figure out how to manage aspects that are part of the growing horizon of memory care. One of our residents, a man in the early stages of dementia, remarked to me that if he had a problem with his heart, he could go to a doctor and get medicine. Then he pointed to his head and asked, "Why can't I go to the doctor and get this fixed?" I really wish I had an answer for him. There is no treatment yet. However, there is care, and we are constantly improving what we offer. Avandell is the next step in dementia living. It is a well-thought-out, enclosed community that allows residents to have freedom and direction over their lives, with professional supervision, medical care, and familiar activities in a normal environment.

CHAPTER 2
LEARNING FROM DE HOGEWEYK™

A few years back, CNN featured Dr. Sanjay Gupta in a segment where he toured De Hogeweyk™ in the Netherlands. This was UMC's first exposure to a revelatory way people could live with dementia. Discussions led to growing and merging Tapestries into Avandell as a new and better way to serve residents and families.

An incredible amount of thinking and experience in memory care went into making De Hogeweyk™ into the successful facility that it is. Dr. Gupta spoke in depth with De Hogeweyk™'s employees, residents, and their families. The video is amazing and enlightening. It really gives you a feel for how well the development team of De Hogeweyk™ designed the inviting village with its colorful buildings, homey interiors, and beautiful outside spaces.

Watching the CNN segment made us realize there was more we could do to take Tapestries to the next level if we could expand its principles to function in a village setting run by UMC. We sought to normalize life for people who are living with a diagnosis of dementia. The current community choices at UMC were not enough and we committed to make practical changes to people's physical environment.

The existing bricks and mortar of our buildings were limiting what we could do if we could only provide a sense of normal living within a safe environment.

I said to my team, "We need to go to Amsterdam and see this!" So, we contacted the De Hogeweyk™ team and arranged an in-depth visit. The staff told us that they had been showing their community to dementia care professionals from all over the world who were as inspired as we were.

The Avandell model incorporated certain aspects of the Dutch approach as we now pioneer new treatments here in the U.S. I'm excited to share a bit more about the inspiration from our journey to De Hogeweyk™ and tell you the elements we took away from the experience.

ORIGINS OF THE DE HOGEWEYK™ DEMENTIA VILLAGE

On paper, De Hogeweyk™ entered the imagination of its founders in 1992. The village campus was completed in 2009 and has been in operation ever since. The origin of De Hogeweyk™ goes further to a broader trend of reimagining what healthcare buildings and a holistic approach to dementia can look like.

For example, the Golisano Children's Hospital at the University of Rochester looks like an "un-hospital." The spaces are designed to be lighthearted and playful. In the hospital, you'll see colorful, wide-open areas with mobiles of giant butterflies, with each floor displaying a different theme, such as parks and water environments. The idea is to make the setting comfortable and sweet by removing the institutional "going to the doctor, and it might hurt" elements.

De Hogeweyk™ was designed with the spirit of happiness and the positivity of living and affirming life. One of the keys to its success comes from a different cultural sensibility that does not dwell on a difference between illness and wellness. In the US, society tends to separate people who have health or mental issues from everyone else. We label them as patients; they are noted as different. The desire to separate and label may have more to do with protecting our own feelings than treating those who need help.

This issue came to the forefront when I learned about a small city in Belgium called Geel, a two-hour drive from De Hogeweyk™. Geel is famous for being a supportive community where people with mental illnesses can live without being judged, mistreated, or locked up.

For centuries, Geel provided an open-door policy for people with schizophrenia and other mental diagnoses. People with these conditions can go to Geel where they can live and move around the town as they please. The actual full-time residents of Geel are accustomed to visitors and residents who are a little bit different. Life is comfortable, and it works out quite well for everyone.

Compared to serious problems the US confronts (or doesn't) in dealing with the mentally ill, a little "Geel thinking" might do us a world of good.

In the spirit of acceptance and joy, De Hogeweyk™ emerged from the tradition of taking a refreshing, different approach to accommodating people with medical conditions and adding positivity to their lives. There is much less separation and assigning labels. The philosophy of "saying yes more than saying no" brings a normal rhythm of life and togetherness instead of setting one group of people apart from others.

LIFE AT THE VILLAGE

One of the main goals of De Hogeweyk™ was to deinstitutionalize traditional dementia care. It's a neighborhood for people with dementia.

At De Hogeweyk™, residents are free to open the doors of their cheerful houses and walk out to any space that is open to them on the site. They are protected and cannot go past the security perimeter. The village provides a wonderful, normal culture where people are encouraged to be themselves. They receive all necessary attention and supervision, which is folded into their day without experiencing anything intrusive.

The difference from traditional facilities that serve people with dementia is that people think that they are home. This is neither false nor fake. What matters is that residents are comfortable and do not have the stress of thinking that they are in an institution.

A De Hogeweyk ™ female resident joined us on our tour. She literally just walked up to us. Eloy, our tour guide, welcomed her and she continued with us on the tour. The entire interaction was normal and lovely. We engaged her in conversation as we continued our tour with Eloy.

De Hogeweyk™ staff are able to supervise in a more relaxed setting because the residents are not compelled to do anything that makes them uncomfortable. People are allowed to be who they are but always with professionally monitored care. People are given a lot of latitude.

On the tour, we learned that a gentleman resident at one of the colorful village resident houses wanted to visit someone at an adjoining house but wouldn't go to the door empty handed. That was not his way. This is an example of how people lived their lives at home and how the village supports the continuation of what was normal to a dementia care resident before he arrived. His upbringing instilled in him that if you visit someone at their home, you bring a little gift. We went with this man to the supermarket. He picked up some cookies and when we went to visit his neighbor, he knocked on their door and asked, "Can I come inside your house? I brought you cookies!"

De Hogeweyk™ Dementia Village showed us an example of normalcy in living one's later years. It made so much sense. We saw a continuation of what people's lives were like before they walked in the door. The culture is to lead with normality. There was no one on the staff saying no. People were encouraged to live their lives the way they had before arriving at their new address. We heard the words "yes" and "of course" all afternoon.

The 180 residents at De Hogeweyk™ live in a four-acre complex that features a town square, hair salon, supermarket, pub, café, and a theater. There are twenty-seven houses, each for six or seven residents. The houses were originally designed to evoke seven different living styles including:

- Living in an urban area
- A formal "aristocratic" Dutch feel
- A more middle-class, tradesperson environment
- An association with Indonesia—a former Dutch colony
- A cozy and homey atmosphere
- A setting for the culturally minded with a love of art, theater, and film
- A place for those with a central religious aspect to life

Each house has its own individual interior design, as well as food and table settings. For example, a more stylized, old-fashioned house features elegant floral wallpaper and antique clocks. Old-style photos and oil paintings adorn the walls. The more modern settings have bright-colored furniture. Even the dishes vary from house to house, depending on the style of the residence.

Since opening, De Hogeweyk™ merged the groups into four different lifestyle house offerings: urban, formal, traditional, and cosmopolitan.

With this breadth of house environments, De Hogeweyk™ is able to make almost every resident feel at home. The site's designers and current staff emphasize Dutch themes, culture, and elements, intended to resonate with Dutch lifestyles.

This focus on Dutch culture may seem like an obvious choice, but as we have seen, people with dementia need regular schedules and simple cues to help them feel comfortable. They count on expecting things not to change with surprises or upgrades. Modern architecture can be so bland and international as to wipe out familiar cultural reference points. De Hogeweyk™ avoids this trap.

As with Avandell, De Hogeweyk™ is not an exercise in fake reality. It's not a Disney set, and no one is trying to fool residents. Staff will not deceive residents about where they are. At a glance, it looks like a small Dutch town, and to a certain extent, it is. The exterior of the buildings are done in a tasteful brick surface in a range of colors.

A courtyard features lines of trees, along with a giant chess set. Benches and tables are all over the place. Residents can walk on the ground level or make their way between parts of the building on overhead walkways. There are mosaic artworks adorning some of the benches. There is greenery everywhere, inside and out.

The look and feel of the houses match with the life experiences of the residents in each house. This is not always perfect, but the intent is to match people of similar backgrounds and values—as if the house were reuniting old friends. De Hogeweyk™ contributes to an atmosphere of normalcy, which is helpful for people with dementia.

The site has an internal space that resembles a market street, complete with a supermarket and hair salon, as well as a restaurant. A wood-paneled café has a piano and wooden bar. Residents can come and go as they wish. They can stop in the grocery store if they want to. In most cases, no money actually changes hands at the register unless it's a family member or visitor making a purchase. Residents can then assist with meal preparation as if they were still in their old homes.

The 250 staff members dress in normal clothing instead of clinical uniforms. All staff members, including those in the café, hair salon, and supermarket, are trained in dementia care. The goal for residents is a relaxed and regular life. However, the space encourages people to develop a routine and stick to it if they so choose.

The hair salon plays an important role in the overall resident's experience, especially for women. When we visited De Hogeweyk™, we observed that having regular appointments at the salon is especially important for women. They are noticeably more relaxed afterward. When women look in the mirror, there is recognition and normalcy. Appearance was a signifier of their identity that had not been lost to dementia.

Due to the nature of dementia, residents will of course have moments of confusion. When this happens, the staff has a number of strategies, including reality orientation and validation therapy, which are forms of psychotherapy focused on immediate, practical problem-solving.

De Hogeweyk™ has been amazing in addressing issues related to dementia care. They have an elevator that automatically activates because De Hogeweyk™ does not assume that residents remember how elevators work. These sorts of plans effectively reduce anxiety and aggression.

Each living style at De Hogeweyk™ has classical or other chosen music for residents that plays in the different houses. Avandell will do something similar because it has been scientifically shown that for dementia residents, music activates the part of the brain that functions the longest. People who can no longer talk can still sing or even play instruments.

Residents at De Hogeweyk™ seem to get more exercise, not from an organized program but mostly from being able to walk about as they want. Freedom of movement also leads to more social contacts, which helps a person with dementia feel more human. Each resident is a person, not a diagnosis.

De Hogeweyk™ puts effort into stimulating residents' minds as well. They have thirty-five different clubs that keep residents active. One is for baking, another for puzzles and, of course, music. Staff will also engage residents in tasks that require some mental effort. A De Hogeweyk™ staff member may ask a resident to clear a single dish from the dinner table and take it to the kitchen. They will not ask for general help clearing the entire table. Any interaction to encourage a resident to participate is based on their capacity. No one is pushed into anything. The idea is to keep them in the rhythm of living and participating.

LESSONS LEARNED

The success of De Hogeweyk™ is undeniable. Before they built the dementia village, the organization had the advantage of operating a traditional nursing home in the same location. Prior to the construction of the new village design, the same population was served and De Hogeweyk™'s management could make comparisons. For example, in 1993, when it was still a regular nursing home, half of the residents were given antipsychotic drugs. In 2015, six years after the village was created, only 8% of residents were given antipsychotics. What a huge improvement.

It is impressive that in a client satisfaction survey completed after opening, De Hogeweyk™ scored 9.1 out of 10, versus 7.5 nationwide. Results like these are not only attributable to the design of the site and its new way of approaching dementia care but also a great deal of the success comes from the breadth of staff, the way they are managed, and the comprehensive training they've received.

There are methods put in place for occasional issues. The social worker at De Hogeweyk™ is known as the go-to person for residents who become angry or disagreeable. Even in such a wonderful environment, these things happen. According to De Hogeweyk™ staff members, a resident even once barricaded himself inside his house. It's an inevitable part of dementia.

When a resident becomes agitated, the social worker has what she calls her "trick book" for certain residents. The trick book contains different approaches to calming down a resident. For instance, if a resident is anxious or getting aggressive, the social worker may go to that person and say excitedly, "I was looking for you!" That usually gets the resident to engage and step back from the confusion and anxiety that was causing them trouble.

Another lesson of De Hogeweyk™ is that the model works best for individuals who are in a certain stage of severe dementia. Their criterion for admission is that a person needs attention and support 24 hours a day.

Living in De Hogeweyk™ has shown that residents are in better physical health than we typically see for a comparable age group in a traditional care setting. This is partly because residents are up and about, walking outside, and getting some exercise. The setting and the way it functions physically and mentally benefits residents, and appetites are more consistent.

When De Hogeweyk™ began, the expectation was that residents would stay for about three years until they passed away. Now the average is about 2.5 years due in large part to the increased acuity level upon admission resulting from the changed rules of the Dutch healthcare policy on nursing home admissions.

The general rule at De Hogeweyk™ is that residents leave when they die. They occasionally place residents into a skilled nursing facility, but for the most part it is a true end-of-life residence. To the extent residents understand this, staff work with residents on this emotionally difficult subject.

One thing to keep in mind is that De Hogeweyk™ exists in a country with a different healthcare model from that of the United States. It cost €19.3 million (about USD $22 million) to build. Most of the funds came from the Dutch government. De Hogeweyk™ receives €5,000 (USD $5,500) per resident per month from the National Dutch Health System, the same amount paid for all Dutch nursing home residents in all facilities. Then, residents are charged €174–€2,500 per month, payable back to the National Dutch Health System based on their ability to pay. This relatively low fee allows residents a .85 to 1 care-staff/resident ratio, which would be impossible to achieve in the US at this level of funding. The nature of socialized medicine and other factors set De Hogeweyk™ and other European facilities apart from those in America.

Now it is up to us to bring the lessons learned from De Hogeweyk™ and adapt them for America with Avandell. Our goal is to provide one of the highest standards of care. We are honored that so many faith-based and secular organizations in the U.S. are interested in following our lead, so they too can change the conversation and culture of the last years of a dementia resident's life.

CHAPTER 3
LIVES IN TRANSITION

I've been working in compassionate senior care for more than forty years. There is no one way to do things, and I learned to be flexible, especially after seeing De Hogeweyk™. History has shown me that although science, history, politics, medicine, and generations change, what doesn't change is our human feelings, our families, and the very basic ways that parents, spouses, children, and grandchildren interact.

Transitions are something that many of us put off but can't escape. This is not just basic human procrastination. We can attribute putting off these major decisions to fear and vanity. An accomplished adult can think that they are immune from the infirmities of aging—because they believe they have *earned* this right.

A common story theme in futuristic science fiction films is the rich CEO trying to buy immortality. Those with means and initiative constantly try to outsmart God, seeking a way to live forever.

A very wise friend of mine who works as a geriatric psychiatrist points out that we grow up in our parents' homes, but we end up living in our children's homes. Inevitably, our health deteriorates. We live longer thanks to medicine and advances in science. We pray for tangible miracles on the horizon as we all continue to get older.

It's interesting when you think of the culture of "our" home of origin versus the culture of our children's homes. There are so many dynamics, along with potential stress and drama, when people exchange parent/child roles. The experience and exploration of family dynamics will impact relationships and inform decisions when planning for any senior living, and the idea of putting off painful decisions does not take into account the level of angst and other emotions that were previously held in check.

You may have noticed the growing number of TV ads for retirement planning and long-term care insurance companies. Policies are advertised on digital media, radio, and print—anywhere advertising exists. There is a growing presence of organizations advertising that they are hiring caretakers and home assistance aids. Agencies advertise that they can arrange payment for a family member to take care of an elder person at home.

The baby boomer generation that has been in denial about aging is surprised and angry as their bodies and minds get older. Boomers expected that "by now" scientific achievements would have saved their generation. "Where are the answers? We were supposed to not have to go through this. We were immune from being burdened with the embarrassment of aging issues!" You can wish as much as you want to, but things just aren't that simple.

Human beings are creatures of habit and denial. We never really think that we will be in a situation of being frail and elderly like the couple living across the street. We say, "That's not going to happen to us. That's never going to be us because we take care of ourselves. We plan for things. We've worked so hard to get where we are, and now we are going to enjoy the fruits of our labor and our retirement years." However, in family after family, we see how people are confronted with the transitions that come with aging. Life has not worked out as hoped for or expected, and the fear about what to do next becomes paralyzing. Many of us will experience our minds beginning to slow down, and we say "We're just getting older," as we become a bit forgetful, especially with names.

Most people don't realize how much they have in common with other families when I get "the phone call." The call that brings people to one of our senior communities typically comes months, or in some cases, years, after the first signs of stumbling over words and situations. These transitions are more common as the population of the United States ages. We are busy and are already managing way too much stress.

In certain societies, people feel shame when they age as they are bombarded with the media's constant celebration of youth. Effectively, we make excuses for the natural aging process because, for many, it feels embarrassing. We don't want to grow old, yet it is inevitable and escapes no one.

Currently, there are over six million Americans living with Alzheimer's disease, which comprises almost 70% of dementia cases. This means that roughly eight and a half million Americans are living with some level of dementia.[1] The current cost of treating Alzheimer's as of 2022 is estimated to be $355 billion. By 2050, the number of Americans with the disease is expected to reach 13 million, with future cost projections of $1.1 trillion.

[1] Alzheimer's Association data - https://www.alz.org/alzheimers-dementia/facts-figures

Dementia is a huge, growing issue affecting our society. Dementia care has also become a business, but for those of us who have dedicated our careers to the field of compassionate care, it has always been much more than that. At UMC, we believe that what will differentiate us from others is how people are treated with-kindness and humanity in our communities. We really care about their quality of life and fulfillment of each day. In Avandell, our goal is to put the person first.

Dementia affects many families, each dealing with their personal challenges in the transition. There are unexpected behaviors and memory loss. We have observed how beneficial it is for elderly people in societies that thoughtfully invest more in taking care of their older populations, especially in the Netherlands and Belgium. We, in the U.S., will have a lot of catching up to do in order to learn about and implement the best care models.

The ability to be a resident of Avandell very much depends on financial means. The U.S. is far from the models we see in the European Union (EU), New Zealand, and Australia—people in America can rely only on their retirement savings, Medicare, Medicaid, and family finances.

I am not here to discuss politics. However, I can tell you that countries have intentionally built secure villages providing happiness and daily living for individuals with dementia. This has inspired me and UMC to deliver the absolute best quality of life for those living in our communities in the U.S. The incredible standards I have seen have made the transition for people to an elder care environment much easier. People are more relaxed in these dedicated dementia villages and can celebrate their retirement in the best possible community setting.

And while there is a growing professional industry set up to help families confronted with dementia, the reality is that a great deal of the care is done by unpaid caregivers—estimated by the Alzheimer's Association to number at least 11 million. These caregivers are usually family members who have no concept of the confusion that has affected the state of their loved one. This is extremely upsetting to the caregiver, who can end up feeling overwhelmed. They are on call twenty-four hours every day doing a job they are neither technically nor emotionally prepared to do.

In sociological studies of different tribes and groups of people in countries other than the United States, for example, Native Americans and the indigenous Inuit, there is a natural expectation and societal acceptance. These cultures always find a way to help an aging parent or grandparent with a built-in, agreed-upon manner of helping the transition. People with these traditions expect that this is the natural course of events without judgment. A cultural process like this may seem old-fashioned or nostalgic, but it has worked throughout most of the history of mankind.

So, what happened? We, as a modern society, reached the stage of mechanical sophistication accompanied by an expectation of instant gratification. Families spread out over countries or continents without thinking through the planning of the aging of older generations. This is especially true in the United States. Technology was supposed to help us, but what it did was rip apart the fabric of community traditions where we take care of our own.

In an earlier era, affluent families hired dedicated, live-in servants that provided critical caretaking roles, and they remained within the family. Today this is rare.

Now to where I come in. I help families accept the reality of what absolutely needs to take place, and I do this with sincerity, patience, and sensitivity. That is my role. Each part of the family, each spoke of the wheel, has independent thoughts and independent needs. I never know family dynamics ahead of these meetings. Family history happened before people walk in to the room. There are often secrets, shame, resentment, guilt, and over-involvement. You just never know. I listen and assess before I say anything. Family dynamics can take over; I need to step back and let them all have their say.

Even though people may live in the same house or work in a particular career for decades, lives are essentially an endless series of transitions. Nowhere is the transition more pronounced than in the final phase. Our bodies age. We become more susceptible to illness and accidents. It is most unfair when our minds begin to deteriorate. This may happen in parallel with a physical decline, but often, the two tracks of existence are far apart, with healthy bodies hosting disappearing minds or mentally aware people witnessing their physical health declining. I will concentrate on the former.

The story I am telling in this book begins with understanding the life transition that occurs as healthy, productive adults begin to undergo profound mental changes.

UNDERSTANDING DEMENTIA AS A DISEASE

Exploration of changes in dementia care should start by defining what it is or what it seems to be—the clinical diagnosis of the neurocognitive disorder (mild, moderate, severe). Dementia is a familiar term, yet the word is no longer found in a formal medical, clinical diagnosis. The reader may try to identify what is happening to the distressed person, but this process is under the auspices of a neurologist.

There are many books on this subject. My goal is to take a moment to help you understand the basics of dementia and the evolving, modern approaches to treatment.

Dementia is not a new phenomenon by any means. Older people can become confused—we knew this but were not always gracious or sensitive to it as a condition. When I was younger, people with dementia were called senile. Even today, families that are trying to cope with upsetting changes joke or trivialize situations due to embarrassment or lack of education about what is happening. Now we understand that dementia is complicated and more nuanced. Science knows more. Just not enough—yet.

It is important to realize that dementia is not a disease; rather, it is a term with broader ramifications. For example, we hear terms such as "kidney disease" or "hardening of the arteries" that can describe a range of specific medical conditions. Dementia can be a result of Alzheimer's disease, the most common form of dementia, but also vascular dementia, Parkinson's-related dementia, Lewy Body Dementia, frontotemporal dementia, alcohol-related, HIV-associated dementia, and many others. Also, Down's Syndrome often leads to Alzheimer's. The National Institutes of Health (NIH) is doing all it can with a myriad of global institutions and genetic researchers to find answers.

Most recently, the NFL, professional boxing and other sports have begun to acknowledge unwelcome responsibility for their roles in not protecting or understanding their athletes who develop CTE, Chronic Traumatic Encephalopathy, through brain trauma. CNN reported on medical research revealing that athletes that have experienced brain trauma had some unexpected consequences such as varying forms of dementia. Brains with CTE show a "disordering" or abnormalities in the brain. In some extreme cases, it can even lead to violent behavior. CTE is often diagnosed only after death in an autopsy.

Dementia results from damage to brain cells, which disrupts the ability to communicate with each other on a micro-cellular level. When this happens, the result is a decline in thinking or cognitive abilities. As dementia progresses, these disorders impair daily life and the ability to function independently.

The degeneration of human biology can also affect emotions and behavior. The negative impact on relationships and communications are by far the most upsetting to family, friends, colleagues, and to patients themselves. As these issues become apparent, we see the tipping point and receive a flood of inquiries regarding available living and care options at UMC.

The symptoms of dementia can be hard to spot, especially early on. Indeed, as we see in case after case, it can be many years until we recognize earlier strange incidents as signs of dementia rather than routine forgetfulness. In our fifties, we all joke about our "senior moments," forgetting names or not remembering why we came into a room. Most of us can backtrack or speak around what word or words elude us. The cascade and frequency of these incidents is the unwelcome change from normal to memory impairment. Dementia symptoms are similar, but they become more frequent and pronounced.

Some early signs of dementia include issues like keeping track of eyeglasses, wallets, and keys. Many people lose the date or day of the week or forget appointments, birthdays, and anniversaries. A particularly distressing symptom is wandering off in "various states of dress," getting lost, or not recognizing a lifelong neighborhood or city landmarks.

For Professor Miller, whom we met in Chapter one, the problem involved getting lost. He drove the same route to work for thirty years, then started to lose his way as he drove home. When it happened once, his wife said, "You were just distracted from a hard day." When it happened again, her personal radar led her to become concerned. When he got lost a third time, a trip that ended with him ramming into a parked car, she realized that this was not a coincidence; it was a problem.

People with dementia can forget to take medication or eat. They can make errors preparing meals and may leave things in the microwave or forget that they have left the gas on while cooking. Action at this juncture is critical because people's lives are at risk. We'll explore this safety factor as we make our way through the book.

Short-term memory disappears and it is apparent when the person living with dementia repeats the same thoughts or asks the same question over and over, often just minutes later, that something is wrong. This forgetfulness is an example of the decrease in the amount of time it takes for a person to repeat the same subject or phrase. The repetition accelerates as a few minutes becomes five, then two, then one minute or less.

Then, they might repeat a sentence in a matter of seconds. These sentences are also a point of reference for a patient. An example would be a parent saying to an adult child, "Do you need money?" This is a natural thing for most parents to say to their young children, but not to an adult child. It is a memory that patients grasp, trying to find a place that can calm them if they feel emotionally or cognitively lost.

Familiar people, including family members, can become strangers. Often the person will talk to or respond to anyone other than a family member, who seems nice or is taking care of him or her. They don't know their names but feel safe with familiar faces. This can be good or not good depending on the living situation and the sort of supervision. Family members become sad at the irony that their parent or loved one truly becomes attached to a caregiver in such a way that a child or spouse no longer is recognized as a positive, loving family member with a depth of history.

Billy Crystal humorously satirized this poignant moment in the film *City Slickers* when he told his son's class that growing old meant spending the end of your life, "Babbling to a nurse your wife can't stand, but you call 'mama.'" Those who take care of the person in need of care see them more often because it is their job. They spend more time together. Children and spouses are not there 24/7.

Family members can feel hurt and might develop a sense of injustice or jealousy. Perhaps the person in care is more docile and dependent and completely different with "strangers" than with their own family. The loved one is truly "living" a new and different life without the memories that family members still have. The brain, not the spirit, is more comfortable with the new environment and constant professional care.

The person does not remember, acknowledge, or appreciate a life with the memories of love and sacrifice from their family. Spending regular time in a non-threatening or non-challenging environment comforts them, and they can be more relaxed around people who neither want nor expect anything from them. There is no intimacy of family interaction, good or not.

This is one of the most difficult things to see, and it is my job to educate families to not take this personally. Easier said than done.

I encourage families to avoid ignoring early signs of dementia. Recognition and early intervention gives everyone the chance to address and perhaps slow down the progression. An early diagnosis gives people choices and a chance to get the maximum benefit from available treatments and ongoing clinical trials. Many medical associations, family advocacy groups, support groups, hospitals, and doctors know about these interventional dementia and Alzheimer's medical trials. Studies may offer treatments and medications that are not available to the general public. Early diagnosis also makes life significantly easier for the caregiver.

THE CONTINUUM OF DEMENTIA

Dementia is a progressive condition that also exists on a continuum of symptoms. Progressive means that symptoms start gradually and then get worse over time. The medical and psychological professions have a number of different ways of categorizing the severity of dementia.

While there are seven levels of dementia, we'll simplify our discussion to mild, medium, and severe.

Mild dementia involves memory problems coupled with difficulty keeping track of time and solving simple life problems. For example, a person with mild dementia might not know to bring his wallet when he's going out on errands. People with mild dementia can usually perform personal hygiene tasks and manage problem-solving for basic needs. Professor Miller, for example, was able to dress himself, eat, and function at home as long as he was interacting only with Judith. The familiarity and routine worked to keep him going.

A turning point for Thomas and Judith happened at a family wedding. Thomas could not recall the names of almost everyone there. People thought it was funny until it wasn't. He ended up wandering alone out of the hotel venue, which could have been a disaster. Thank goodness the police found him after a three-hour search as he walked along the side of a road in an unfamiliar town.

Moderate dementia is a level where issues become more obvious and pronounced. People with moderate dementia tend to become easily disoriented regarding time and place. They have major memory loss. Their long-term memory stays stronger while short-term memory ebbs away. People know names and faces through photographs and videos. They know their nostalgic favorite films and movie stars. This material and their experiential memories are what make up their life's context that defined their living history. Ironically, the old memories, so far back in time, are easier to recall.

Professor Miller always had great, natural recall—he was a leading scientist. Thomas remembered almost everything when speaking about his childhood in the 1930s and 1940s Brooklyn, New York, but he no longer knew where he presently lived nor the date, day, or year.

The Petersons, another nice family we worked with, shared an anecdote about her mother's shift from mild to moderate dementia. By the time Kathleen Peterson was eighty-one, her daughter Susan was helping navigate the challenges of early dementia. Her mother was confused and forgetful, but her functioning was not all that bad. She could engage in conversations and take part in many of her regular activities.

Kathleen's notable transition was revealed at a neurologist appointment that included a mental status exam. The doctor asked her to draw a clock. Her mother was unable to draw a clock's face as Susan watched in horror and choked back tears.

"She drew a circle," Susan explained. "And then, she stopped. She couldn't remember what went inside the circle. She tried to put in numbers, but they were in the wrong places. Then she couldn't draw the hands or decide where 12, 1 and 2 should have been."

This was the moment that Susan realized her mother needed more help than she was giving her.

So, it was time—Kathleen obviously needed more help at home. She could not be as independent as she had been, and Kathleen lost interest in many of the things she had previously enjoyed, like playing bridge with friends and gardening. This is what moderate dementia looks like.

A spouse, or in this case, Susan, the adult child, begins to truly lose the person they once knew. The person is still in there, but it can be difficult to see a loved one through the mask of the illness.

Severe dementia is a state of severe memory loss and nearly total disorientation. There are almost zero cognitive reference points with this level of memory loss. People with severe dementia may hardly ever speak. Their problem-solving abilities are gone, so they become completely dependent on another's care. They can enjoy certain activities, such as listening to music but cannot focus on a television screen or chat with anyone as to what the program is about. They require help with nearly all tasks of daily living including dressing, toileting, and basic personal hygiene.

Incontinence is almost always part of this stage of dementia, requiring constant attention to a person's comfort, wetness/dryness, and risk of infection or skin irritation. This is medically necessary. Having to monitor them can be difficult enough for all levels of staff in senior memory care facilities, let alone for a spouse, child, or grandchild doing their best to care for an elder relative. People with severe dementia cannot articulate what they need or what they are feeling. For example, they cannot communicate if they have pain.

In addition to the multiple stages of dementia, the specific impacts of the illness can differ from case to case. This is because the brain has distinct regions, and each can be affected by the brain cell damage inherent in dementia. One person might have her memory most affected. For someone else, it can be movement, speech, or impaired judgment.

Managing the mind and the body is essential. There can be a myriad of additional health problems, such as depression and anxiety. Falling for different reasons becomes more common. The person may be at risk for stroke, deep vein thrombosis (DVT), urinary tract infections, the inability to remember to swallow food or saliva, loss of motor skills, and "acting out" in anger.

In the end, the person may stop eating—a moment that, in my experience, may signal that someone no longer wants to go on living. Death usually follows within a short period of time.

The duration of these stages varies greatly from person to person. In some cases, the entire cycle can last less than a year. Other individuals, depending on their general level of health and fitness, who are diagnosed with early onset in their fifties or sixties, may live a longer life. People can live one or two decades more than expected if they receive superior care or have the good fortune to have been born with good genes. **What ties all these people together, when it comes to living as full a life as possible, is that we meet them where they are and treat them with kindness and care.**

WHY DEMENTIA IS AN INCREASINGLY SERIOUS ISSUE TODAY

While dementia appearing as we grow older is not new there is now a greater challenge for families and society at large—things are changing for a number of reasons. Most notably, people are simply living longer. Until the middle of the last century, it was not uncommon to pass away at sixty to seventy-five years of age before dementia could become an issue. Today, with improved medical care and prescription medications, physical therapy, eating better, and taking vitamin and mineral supplements, people are living longer.

The "shift in the paradigm" of now, a longer life, has benefits and downsides. It is wonderful that so many people can live long, fulfilling lives. I certainly hope, with God's grace, that I enjoy that privilege. We see that a billion-dollar anti-aging industry has risen up, offering false hope—or at a minimum, some misguided thinking on what it means to become old. I meet many people today who seem to think they can avoid growing old, wanting to live forever, as I suggested earlier. These are modern versions of literature's notorious Dorian Gray.

Society has solutions to provide comfort in one's elder years, with assisted living and group homes, senior centers, and professional and community programs specific to enhance daily life for the older generation. Senior centers offer games like Scrabble and bridge to keep the mind active. They are dedicated to providing nutrition and regular exercise, including ballroom dancing, yoga, tai chi, and water and chair aerobics, which help the quality of physical, spiritual, and emotional life. Better healthcare at an older age means that many people live long enough for their minds to deteriorate even as their bodies remain healthy. The bittersweet result of "healthier elderly people," however, is a substantial need for millions of people to seek dementia care. This is a growing trend and challenging for everyone involved.

DEMENTIA'S IMPACT ON FAMILIES

A person with dementia can have a profound effect on everyone in his or her family circle. The types and severity of dementia add to the impact on existing circumstances, which vary greatly from one family to another, often relating to the ages of the people involved, family dynamics, and relationships prior to the onset of dementia. Family members may have their own families. There could be plans in place for university, career moves, and personal commitments. The person may have children with special needs. Limits due to geography, availability, willingness, and money are all factors weighing on how to proceed with the best care possible for a loved one.

As a spiritual mentor of mine once said, "Each single family is different because each human being is different. Valuable spiritual insights come from understanding the dignity of difference." To me, this means that because no two people are alike, no two responses to treating and managing dementia will be alike. Every family is going to experience their own, unique transition factors. The valuable lesson here is to respect that all involved will have a personal and sometimes very different understanding based on present perceptions, family history, and dynamics—and their own life situations.

DEMENTIA AND THE MARRIED COUPLE

The Millers offer a good example of how dementia affects a married couple. Judith and Thomas were married for forty years, and their marriage was always challenging, now more so. They both worked in the sciences and Judith agreed to lessen her career goals so that the Professor could follow his career track that would lead to professional and personal fame. Somehow, the couple figured out how to make it work. It wasn't easy. I only mention this because the onset of dementia can amplify issues (good or bad) that already exist in a marriage or any close relationship as much as it creates its own new problems.

Thomas's career grew to great success. He ran the Astrophysics Department at a major university and was in demand as a speaker. He published. He traveled. He developed significant aspects of the Large Hadron Collider (the world's largest and highest-energy particle collider) at CERN. Thomas was always proud and happy to pick up the check when going out to dinner or vacationing with friends.

Judith told me that she realized something was going on and changing with Thomas when he was giving a speech at a large event. At one meeting, the man sitting next to him, a longtime colleague and someone he had known for years, was with him on the platform. When Thomas started to acknowledge the man, he drew a blank of his famous friend's name. Even within the unease, everyone laughed at the "senior moment." That's what we do.

If he couldn't get a thought out, he might shift to a totally different topic. But his default would be to find some safety in topics that were familiar and referencing very familiar subjects of conversation to save the moment.

Thomas understood that something was wrong, so he downloaded Scrabble and Words with Friends on his laptop, phone, and tablet. He also enrolled in a memory and aging program at a local hospital that used the data in an ongoing study. His abilities did not worsen, and no further decline was observed from that point.

He didn't display any of the classic markers of dementia. A few years went by, and still, nothing changed. This can be very common. In fact, this is that sort of "middle zone" where symptoms get missed, and incidents are attributed as one-offs.

Then things really started to change for the worse. Thomas had a few incidents where he lost his way while driving. He was forgetting important conversations with colleagues or his family that had taken place within the past two weeks. He had friends from his social organizations who did not understand why once in a while Thomas would lose his way in the middle of telling relevant stories or when mentoring and offering advice to younger members of a group.

Thomas continued to forget names. More often, he seemed mentally paralyzed—definitely stuck or repetitive. He would have a conversation and lose the context and subject matter, trying to remember what had been said and making references to other unrelated subjects that made no sense.

Thomas became even more repetitive, asking questions or saying things two or three times within a very short period of time. Before dementia, he had always been incredibly witty—able to switch gears and keep up with multiple conversations at dinner tables and professional meetings.

That was when Thomas decided to retire. He never said it, but I believe he was gently forced to retire by the university. He was only in his early seventies, not old by today's standards, but he could not function in his job any longer, and he stopped traveling to Switzerland to consult on the famous machine he once helped to build and develop.

The Millers went back to the hospital for tests. The neurology department scheduled him for a cognitive exam, an MRI, and a PET scan. Results showed that some amyloid had, developed in his brain. There was something going on. Thomas was now officially diagnosed with early-stage Alzheimer's disease. This was, for him, a gut punch.

Judith was the first person to observe the progression. "He would either keep saying the same thing every thirty seconds or just talk, talk, talk . . . going from one subject to another," she said. "It was very hard to follow him."

He started losing mail and misplacing his wallet, yet Thomas was still able to pay the bills and seemed to mostly function. Then he stopped remembering scheduled financial responsibilities. Collection warnings started to arrive in the mailbox. Judith also discovered that he double paid or thought he had double paid other bills. It became a mess.

Thomas started asking friends and strangers for money. Friends asked Judith, "Is everything okay? Thomas just asked to borrow a thousand dollars." It progressed, and Thomas started to become belligerent and accuse friends and family of taking his money, or he claimed people had promised to lend him money. This was embarrassing for Judith, not only because they didn't need any money but also now other people knew about their private family secret. Something was wrong with Thomas.

This was a turning point for Judith herself. Thomas's dementia was taking a toll on her. She was in the middle of the "storm," as we call it, and had lost perspective regarding her own life. Lately she had spent endless hours taking care of Thomas and dealing with his memory and money matters. Thomas was her full-time job, and on top of that, they had a house, meals needed to be prepared, and taxes were almost due. She was understandably exhausted and not equipped to manage symptoms of dementia in her husband within her own home. She had a level of denial that this was really happening. In spite of her skill juggling many demanding tasks, her own career, and being Mom and wife to her husband and children, admitting to the magnitude of Thomas's illness would be for her a "weakness."

DEMENTIA'S IMPACT ON FAMILIES WITH ADULT CHILDREN

When we first met the Petersons, we were introduced to Kathleen and her daughter, Susan, who was caring for her mother. However, before Kathleen displayed symptoms, her husband, William, had his own early onset dementia and passed away due to another physical problem, cancer.

William's symptoms had been in the mild category, and the family was relieved that they could handle small memory missteps. We've talked about the most common experience of denial when it comes to the relief of not yet having to make any life-changing decisions. Of course, people prefer to minimize the situation without considering what may happen until things become serious. It is mourning before mourning.

When William died, Kathleen was in her late sixties and had her own small memory issues, but they did not become problematic for another nine years. Her two adult children, Susan and Jack Peterson, were in their forties and encouraged Kathleen to take up hobbies of stimulating games, such as Sudoku or the New York Times crossword puzzles. At first, she refused. William had always been her partner when she did the crosswords.

Nine years after her husband passed away, Kathleen's mild dementia symptoms were becoming problematic. Action was needed. Susan and Jack never expected that what happened to their father would then affect their mother, who had her own version of denial. The progression of dementia symptoms had been so sneaky. It was hard to say when Kathleen's issues became worse. This is completely understandable and quite common.

Kathleen was embarrassed by her diagnosis. We see embarrassment and shame from the diagnosis more often than you might think. Instead of accepting a diagnosis as a medical issue, Kathleen saw her condition as a weakness of character; a personal defect, or a lack of inner strength.

Though irrational, it is relevant to note that a part of us tries to say to the person, "Do something! Don't let this happen. Snap out of it." All these feelings of anger around the diagnosis of their loved one come out. Family members ask doctors for symptoms to be "fixed." Medical professionals need to be sensitive to all people involved in appointments or consultations because different people react in different ways.

The diagnosis of dementia, which is not a specific or single disease, can be related to various mental and physical conditions through the Central Nervous System (CNS), which consists of the brain and spinal cord. Various types of dementia, along with Alzheimer's disease, are not conditions a patient can choose to turn off. The only choices available are those involved in planning how to live and manage while a patient is alive. We cannot choose to go backward and be the people we once were when the brain and body are attacking our capacity to function.

For Kathleen, who was aging when her husband was fading into dementia, she felt resentful and powerless. His dementia signaled her own mortality, which she was not ready to confront. She barely had the energy to deal with her husband's case. Nor was she ready to think about life alone. Susan and Jack were not eager to accept their father's deterioration. He had been such a major figure in their lives, and every day, he was less able to function. The family had underestimated the situation and were in "wish mode," constantly looking for things to be the way they had been.

Then, William got cancer. I would never say that being diagnosed with an additional, serious disease is a blessing, but in this case, his illness somehow helped the family to deal with their father's decline. After William passed away, Kathleen made an important decision, which was to move nearer to Susan and Jack, who both lived in close proximity to one another a few hours from their original hometown.

The best decision made by Kathleen was that she and William worked with a financial planner and insurance specialist. They were organized and planned ahead, which I encourage families to consider as early as possible. Kathleen selected a continuing care retirement community that was designed for transitioning into elder care. She chose a nice condominium in the gated neighborhood, knowing that there was assisted living and skilled nursing, along with dementia care available for her if needed.

As Susan realized that Kathleen began to have more memory issues and problems, she again brought her mother to the neurologist. Tests revealed more signs of progression. She was still able to live on her own with a housekeeper companion helping out a few days per week.

Then, as Susan put it, "We knew it was time to put Mom's plan into action," when there were more serious memory events, and now her mother was exhibiting anxiety, depression, and some panic attacks. These attacks were really difficult to identify because they resembled heart attacks.

"And," Susan explained, "she would call me at all hours of the day, not knowing where she was. She couldn't remember conversations we'd had that day and had total memory loss about certain experiences." She never got to the point where she stopped recognizing her children, but her short-term memory was gone, and remembering became impossible.

"It just started to cascade," Susan added. "I was visiting or checking on her once or twice a week until she started demanding I drive over. We started talking about having in-home help, which she really didn't want, but knew that she'd rather have company than constantly be scared."

Susan and Jack had a fairly good relationship, and caring for their mother did not present a major inconvenience. Money was not a big issue, and their career parameters were flexible. They could spend time with their mother at a moment's notice. Most families don't have the luxury of having these choices and options.

In fact, dementia can, unfortunately, elicit all sorts of bad sibling behavior and propel toxic family dynamics into high gear. I've seen situations where one child is scheming to get money from the parents or clearly stealing. Often an unmarried child will take on the lion's share of parental care and logistics because that sibling doesn't have as many people to look after. This impinges upon a grown child being able to live a full life, and the dynamic is ripe for sibling arguments and resentments.

Susan and Jack decided that it would be best if Kathleen would transition and begin spending her days in the memory care neighborhood; she and William had planned for this. Kathleen knew that was her "other nice, comfortable place" and was allowed to be there.

"We said, 'if you're not going to have somebody at home, how about spending the days where people are available if you need something,'" said Jack.

It was reassuring that, if Kathleen wandered around, became confused, or felt worried, there were always professionals there who knew how to be kind and pleasant in a moment of fear.

Susan shared, "I would take my mom there around eight in the morning so she could engage with the other residents. Then I'd pick her up in the eveninng, have dinner with her, and bring her back to her house."

"She really didn't want it," said Susan, "but she slowly started to realize that she needed it."

CHAPTER 4

MOVING BEYOND DENIAL: THE MOMENT OF REAL FAMILY CRISIS

"Get out of my house," Kathleen screamed at her daughter, Susan, standing in the doorway. Earlier in the day, Susan took her mother to a follow-up neurological status exam, which was definitive. Kathleen was furious because it went badly and she was still able to understand much of what the doctor had said about her dementia.

Kathleen showed much confusion during the test. When they got home and walked from the garage, Kathleen dug in and blamed Susan. As the saying goes, "We always hurt the ones we love." This can especially be the norm when people with dementia lose their sense of appropriate levels of interaction and control of their emotions.

Kathleen always had a tendency to blame her loved ones when she was angry and frustrated, as human beings do, except now, her usual anger episode was magnified to a critical level. Susan had never seen her mom so disturbed and out of control as Kathleen pushed Susan out the door, slammed it shut, and locked every lock.

This last neurological exam was the turning point and pushed Kathleen's temper into overdrive. Susan really couldn't make excuses for her mother's behavior to others. She wanted to believe that she could handle this and figure things out. She was strong and would find the perfect formula. Everything was going to be okay. But it was not okay and now Susan had to begin the process of acceptance.

Susan was shattered when her mother locked the door. As caretaker and daughter, Susan took charge of managing Kathleen's continuing mental decline. This had been the day that her mom couldn't draw a clock. Susan described this moment to me as "a beacon of fear." Susan didn't resent having to take care of her mother, but unfortunately, she was putting her own life priorities on hold. Caring for her mother had turned into a 24/7 endeavor.

At the exam, Kathleen did not know what month it was, and she had recently had her second minor car accident within four weeks of the first one. Susan explained to the doctor that her mother often forgot there had been not only one accident but two. The signs that her life was changing were frightening. She was aware that her life would never be the same.

Caretakers come to us physically shaken. They often cannot catch their breath when trying to articulate the magnitude of what is going on. Caretakers frequently manage their own physical and mental problems that manifest as anxiety, stress, and depression.

At UMC, we have these conversations most days of the week. Not only do we assess the person's status, we also counsel spouses, children, partners, or friends who themselves are mentally and physically running on fumes.

Dementia takes its toll on everyone. We hope that there is a moment of realization early enough by families so that everyone involved in decision-making does not get to the point of being incapacitated. It is challenging to talk to a paralyzed, angry, embarrassed, exhausted, and grieving family. UMC is prepared for these family dynamics. Again, our job is to help and be kind. We understand.

There also are people with the most common types of dementia, such as vascular dementia and Alzheimer's disease, who usually have a mild form of aphasia—not being able to speak or find that words continually escape them. Dementia can progress and can increase the frequency and severity of aphasia. People with dementia who experience aphasia try to speak or have a conversation, which leads to frustration and sometimes sadness or anxiety.

Kathleen had some lucid moments when she felt as though she had control, yet her fading reality gave her a feeling that there was always some sort of impending danger when she went about her day, performing regular activities. Susan knew that things were getting worse. Her mother's innate anger became uncontrollable enough that she could not look away or take the chance that Kathleen could do harm to herself or others.

After the exam, the doctor took Susan aside and said, "Your mother shouldn't be driving, and she definitely should not be living alone." When Susan tried to explain to Kathleen the previous week that she would no longer be allowed to drive, Kathleen exploded and was inconsolable. Susan felt like she was mourning for the mother she once knew.

At UMC, we are guided by the principle of living the life you love. It is so important that caregivers understand that they have the right to their lives. The diagnosis has a reciprocal effect on caregivers. Family members also want to live the lives they love, but this is really difficult when mild dementia progresses to different levels of moderate.

Here is the family's crisis moment that can't be ignored. It doesn't always occur when a family is caring for a parent with dementia, but it's common enough that I view it as almost inevitable. Providing care at home becomes challenging to the point of impossibility. Many times, we see a spouse who becomes physically ill from the strain of all things that happen to the body as we age.

A decision needs to be made. Where can this person get the best care and live the life they love to the extent that it is possible?

Making this decision can be agonizing for even the healthiest of families. Children feel guilt about placing their parents in dementia care. Parents may feel betrayed, and the sincere, earlier promises to keep the parent at home may no longer be able to be honored. So many families must confront and then accept that things can only get worse unless a concrete decision is made. We are here to help them.

THE POINT OF IMPOSSIBILITY

Sometimes, the decision to place a loved one in an eldercare community is the result of an earlier, agreed-upon plan initiated by the one with dementia with their legal advisor or chosen power of attorney. That is a preferred scenario if a family is in a position, based on family dynamics, to have discussions and include the person with dementia. Facing reality is hard.

Care decisions are often brought up in estate, financial, and insurance planning with a professional during a time when people are more likely to be under less pressured circumstances. A person of clearer mind is in a better position to make conscientious, personal decisions.

Arriving at a care plan decision is daunting. I've mentioned that many other factors may affect the dynamics in a family meeting. Each person involved and each family is different. There will be so much emotion due to history, finances, present circumstances and experiences of transition affecting the conversation. Frustration can be the factor that ends the conversation, so we often must start again from the beginning on another day. This is how so many families we work with have to make decisions after they've reached what I call "the point of impossibility."

Dementia is progressive, so at a certain point, care at home invariably becomes too difficult. The situation is especially unsafe for all involved. If you try to make home "easier" for the person, the well-meaning gesture can backfire and cause confusion. This is true even for families with ample financial resources who can afford in-home caregivers. The average American house or apartment is not equipped to handle caring for a person with dementia. Many problems are built into the design and security of the dwelling.

We spoke with one quite affluent family. They had the financial capability to retain round-the-clock caregivers for their ninety-one-year-old father with vascular dementia, however, the man's eighty-one-year-old wife was reluctant to have outsiders in the house. She wanted to remain the primary caregiver, which was negatively affecting her health.

She had to make many daily decisions that were stressful and exhausting. At any moment, anything could change, and her resilience was waning. She was the only person her husband still knew and trusted. He only let her cut his hair and his food; everyone else was a stranger. Her husband often became disoriented and terribly frightened. Within a year, she was hospitalized for cardiac issues from the stress.

With their mother in the hospital, the couple's two adult children, each with careers and families of their own, had to drop everything and fly in to take over their father's caregiving. What made things particularly challenging was that they did not know his routine and their mother's carefully honed coping mechanisms or solutions to manage their father's mood swings. They did not know the details of his day-to-day regimen, which their mother had been orchestrating on an incredibly detailed level to make even one hour go smoothly.

It was now more than apparent that their mother was exhausted, and no one knew what to do. Or, they knew, but they did not want to know.

When their mother came home from the hospital, she continued with her previous home caregiving duties for her husband, but she agreed to delegate more by hiring a full-service home care agency. She let go of trying to control everything, which she had done selflessly, with love.

Many times an elderly couple can cope well together but not separately. The couple had known each other so well, for so long, that one of the spouses could compensate for the other's issues. But apart, neither of them can function effectively. Put it this way: I say "1+1 = 1."

In our meeting, a family anecdote came up that her husband, a World War II veteran, had years earlier often said, "If I become senile, just dump me at the VA." This family chose UMC for their father, even though the VA takes very good care of veterans, offering well-trained professional and caring staff. In this gentleman's case, UMC was the preferred option.

The need for a decision about care most often is the result of a crisis, which clarifies to a family or a partner that care for their loved one at home is no longer a feasible option. It could be a mother's hospitalization, as in the last example, or it could be a behavioral outburst that overloads everyone's ability to deal with situations.

We worked with a family whose father, Bob, had once been known as the sweetest man in the world. His dementia put him in a state of mind that changed his personality to the absolute opposite end of the "nice" spectrum. The cold and cantankerous version of their lovely father was heartbreaking, and no one knew how to cope with this man they had never known. He was now angry and impatient.

One day, Bob slipped out of the house when his wife was in the kitchen. He ended up in the office of the church where he had been a lay leader for decades. Everyone in the office knew him. Unfortunately, he started yelling at them and using really bad language. This was an absolute departure and not the Bob they knew.

The church office called his wife who came over and simply said, "Bob, it's time for lunch."

He replied, "Oh? Okay."

He instantly calmed down, and they left peacefully. This was his wife's last straw. Bob could no longer be at home.

Susan Peterson's arrival at the point of impossibility came as Kathleen required almost constant supervision, protection, and redirection to get through her day. Kathleen's issues also started to affect Susan's and Jack's own families.

Susan's children, who were by then in college, couldn't bear being around their grandmother. They were devastated. The grandmother didn't quite know who they were, which upset them. Again, this is a situation I have seen many times over the years. Young people don't have the life experience to understand aspects of dementia, especially when it affects someone they once felt close with.

Kathleen's case is unusual, though, because, according to her kids, she had not been especially affectionate throughout her life. Dementia had made her more cuddly. She was now into giving hugs and putting her arm around people. Not the way she used to be.

On the other hand, dementia accelerated Kathleen's anxiety. At one point, she called 911 because she was worried the loud rain would collapse her roof. The local police had Susan's number on file from a previous "wandering" episode, so Susan was able to deal with the situation and reassure her mother.

"She developed so much anxiety," Susan said. "About everything. She never forgot my phone number, and she started calling all the time about dangers she imagined all around the house. She was constantly confused, and she felt like she had to do things. She would call me out of pure fear. I think that Mom was scared because she recognized that she didn't have a grasp of what was going on."

During the day, Kathleen would walk from room to room and open drawers. She sometimes hid things, like wrapping up money in Kleenex and stashing it around the house. She did that with her jewelry as well. She would hide photos in random books. Then she started pacing room-to-room, looking through things. There was always a concern about her belongings. She worried that things were not in the right place or she had lost something.

For the Millers, their critical moment manifested in family finances. Thomas, the former professor, had taken care of the bills and all the banking for their entire marriage. Their generation grew up in a different time, and that was their way of doing things.

At a certain point in the progression of his dementia, however, it became clear to Judith that she would need to take over financial responsibility.

It is interesting that, like Kathleen Peterson, Thomas was cognitively healthy enough to recognize and understand what was going on but not cognitively capable of seeing WHY it was necessary.

He reacted badly. He felt something was being unfairly taken away from him. "That was the start of a very uncomfortable time," Judith related to me later. "I had to constantly convince Thomas to trust me—that he wasn't losing independence, but he felt insecure and paranoid. This is one of the things that made him interrogate people, saying they were taking his money or that they owed him money."

The financial matters were really just one layer of an increasingly difficult situation for Judith, as she became stressed out and fatigued—the pattern of spousal exhaustion we have been discussing. She was younger than Thomas, who was eighty-five, and she was in her late seventies at this point. She had to make a decision about what to do about him and them.

PRACTICALITIES

Judith's situation shows the commonalities of how things often progress. The practicalities of caring for someone with dementia are many, and they can be quite challenging, especially for someone who is also aging.

Here are two (slightly) humorous anecdotes to illustrate the moment: The first story involved my doctor, who said he once watched as two elderly men came into his waiting room. One said to the other, "You sit over there now and be quiet. Don't make a fuss. I'm going to talk to the lady at the desk." The doctor was baffled by this exchange until he found it was a father and son. The father was ninety-five, the son, seventy-five. The relationship dynamics had never changed. The father did not have dementia, but we can only imagine what the relationship would have been if he did have those issues.

Another reminder of the realities of aging came up a few years ago when an elderly man came to visit our offices to learn about our services. He seemed frail, and I simply assumed he was looking at our community for himself. After talking for a while, he said, "Well, I think my mother will like it here." What? He was in his early eighties. His mother was well over 100.

Not all stories are funny, though. Our population now has a syndrome we call "elder orphans." We will see this more often among aging baby boomers than with previous generations. Some people have outlived their family members. Perhaps they never had children. These people manage on their own until they can't. In some cases, they understand their situation and make plans and arrangements on their own. However, we have had calls from concerned neighbors and law enforcement asking, "Can you do something about this person? He's all alone and becoming demented. He needs to be living in a facility."

The Petersons arrived at a good practical solution, but it didn't last. They placed an ad in the local college paper and found a young woman, Maria, who was interested in social work and elder care, to work a few hours every day to help their mother. "We didn't need skilled nursing," said Jack. "We just needed somebody to check on her every day." People who have multiple helpers or family living nearby are much more likely to cope better and stay at home longer than those who don't have the option for these resources.

Kathleen and Maria hit it off. The visits became what Susan and Jack called "Camp Maria." They would go out together and get manicures. Maria helped make lunch and they would go on short outings. Maria was at the house a few times per week and updated Susan and Jack via email or text. She let them know Kathleen's status and whether there was anything to be concerned about. Maria would take photo selfies of the two of them in the park or on a walk. She would also help monitor and pick up Kathleen's prescriptions, making sure she was taking them as prescribed.

Over time, though, Kathleen's needs outstripped Maria's skills and availability. She was almost done with college and was looking for a job. Around this time, it became clear that Kathleen needed twenty-four-hour care. The brother and sister had to make a family decision.

EMOTIONAL REALITIES

For some, moving a loved one to an elder care facility can be emotionally devastating. For many reasons, the resident feels emotionally traumatized. People with dementia don't deal well with change, especially changes in living situations. They don't deal well with the move. Even if the person is experiencing later stages of dementia, they are getting the point—this is the final stage of their lives.

For children and spouses, moving a family member into elder care often triggers feelings of guilt and shame. This is understandable. A spouse or a child may feel obligated to take care of the person with dementia. He or she may not be able to admit that it has all become too much to handle. This is not a failure, but it can feel that way. It can feel like giving up.

There is the perception that a nursing home is a terrible place to be. No child or spouse would want that for someone they love. Indeed, one of the founders of the De Hogeweyk™ dementia village in Holland, which inspired our new Avandell project, spent her career as a nurse in a nursing home. When her father died suddenly, she explained that she felt a great sense of relief that he would never have to live in a nursing home. The revelation surprised her, and she was inspired and wanted to pioneer a new, better way of doing things.

There have been so many positive advances in elder care, but a fear of nursing homes still persists in society. Kathleen Peterson used to remind Susan and Jack with her message of guilt, "When I married your father, it was 'til death do us part,' and I expect you to make the same promise to me. You must promise you'll never put me in a horrible nursing home!" What a thing to say to your children!

According to Jack, even when his mother had become quite cognitively impaired, she was razor sharp about this directive. He said, "We'd be watching TV, and she would be confused about what day it was and where she was. A commercial for assisted living would come on, and she would snap right out of it and say, 'You promised you'd never do that to me. Right?'"

The Millers had a comparable but different experience. Issues in their marriage surfaced when dealing with the decision to move Thomas into a dementia community. Judith was the problem solver of the family. She needed to be needed, and she was so good at taking care of her family. Judith needed purpose and was holding back on letting go. Yet there is always a limit to one's capacity to deal with impossible challenges. Judith was forced to confront her own limitations and do what was best for them both in their relationship.

One thing that made it a bit easier was that her husband was no longer himself. Rabbi Jeffrey Sirkman says, and he is correct, "The person is still there, deep inside, but the practical day-to-day experience may render this insight irrelevant in practical terms. This is because the loved one is truly living in the moment and does not have the need for the constant attention and help that they were used to before losing their cognitive functions."

Rabbi Sirkman also had a suggestion for families who are coping with the pain of dealing with a loved one with dementia. The husband of a couple in his congregation became severely demented in a relatively short period of time. It became impossible for his wife to care for him, so she decided to arrange a room in a nearby memory care community. Before the gentleman was moved, the rabbi arranged for him to be part of a special, holy ceremony that was integral to the observance of the annual Jewish holidays. The rabbi helped the family create a new memory and honor the man. The ceremony marked a joyous moment and helped create a final, positive memory of the husband that would stay with his wife after he moved into the community. She was so very grateful for this, and the experience added so much meaning to the entire experience of transition. Perhaps we should think about how we can add positivity and love during these transitions for everyone.

MAKING THE DECISION

Depending on the dynamics of the family and the severity of the dementia, at some point, a decision needs to be made. There are many different ways to start. The best approach is to involve the person with dementia to the greatest extent possible. They may not be aware of everything that's happening, but they are definitely sensitive to big changes. If they are gently told and able to understand that they are going to be living somewhere else, that's best.

For people who are still in early dementia, it can be very difficult. They may not accept that they can no longer live at home. Frequently, they don't understand how difficult it is to care for them. That is one of the unfortunate impacts of the disease. They don't see the strain they're causing. Indeed, they may perceive the decision to have them live in assisted living or memory care as an affront to their dignity, or perhaps they feel abandoned.

In my experience, however, even if there is tension around the decision, it will probably be accepted. Sometimes the person will allow family and a care community to bring them to a new place. However, we know of a gentleman with early-stage dementia who was moved into a care facility after his wife passed away. His family could not take care of him, and he had a regimen of medications that were absolutely necessary. The man found a way out of a rather secure facility in the middle of the night and walked home. This can be heartbreaking for everyone, residents, families, and caregivers.

I think that people understand, deep down, what is happening. Usually, the move can represent an improvement in their day-to-day lives. We have developed a community that is ready for any eventuality and will approach the person and the family with the utmost respect and understanding. Yes, everyone is different. We worked hard to develop standard procedures and suggestions based on what we know when it is time to move someone into our communities. We can pivot when necessary. All of this is to make the person feel safe and welcomed.

Making the actual move can be tricky. There are so many different scenarios we have seen. The staff is always informed of a new person joining the community and have things they can do if the new resident is in need of comfort or something to take away the distress, like an activity or a walk in a butterfly garden.

The Petersons got lucky because Maria, the woman who had been so helpful as Kathleen's aide, was doing an internship at the memory care facility where Kathleen would move to.

They told their mother, "We're going to have lunch with Maria today," at the senior living community. Kathleen enjoyed seeing Maria for lunch and was in a good mood. When they asked their mom if she was happy and comfortable staying there, she said, "yes." She was happy that Maria was there. This was a good solution, and Maria was the one who actually took over for the rest of the day to get Kathleen settled in.

THE IMPORTANCE OF PLANNING

These stories show that if there can be an agreement in a family about what to do in advance of someone becoming affected by dementia, it is for the best. Planning is critical if it can be done. This includes managing legal documents such as wills and trusts, as well as living wills, do-not-resuscitate (DNR) orders and powers of attorney.

After someone develops dementia, it's much harder, if not impossible to get a true sense of what they want. The plan can change, of course. It is so valuable to have a sense of what someone wants before they become unable to express themselves. Have the conversation. It takes courage but will pay off emotionally for everyone involved.

The good news today is that there are many new options for care. Avandell will be the latest. Even now, seniors can choose to live in communities that include independent living, assisted living, and memory care. With these choices available, a family can start the transition process into care before a crisis occurs and the decision results in stress and emotional fallout.

How many times have I heard a new resident say, once they've settled in, that they "should have moved in years ago." Or a family member says how mom or dad has "perked up" since moving into one of our communities. Many times this is due to the social isolation they were experiencing at home. Maybe they weren't eating correctly or getting the necessary nutrition at home because there was too much to manage. Once these issues are resolved, people can thrive in senior living communities. We want people to be happy and live their best lives because life is precious.

CHAPTER 5

WHAT ARE THE CURRENT OPTIONS FOR SENIORS?

I would like to give you an overview of the current options available to U.S. families, partners, and friends helping their loved ones as they age. This chapter reviews the most common choices available. Not all of them are suitable for the Miller or Peterson families at their stages of dementia and unique, personal journeys.

Information is empowerment, and it is important to have a sense of senior care options and how things work. Understanding the industry and how eldercare is currently practiced will help you better appreciate the Avandell concept. Hopefully, the difference may help you figure out what's best for your family situation.

There are two essential categories of eldercare; either care provided by the family or professional care options. The Millers and the Petersons have moved beyond family-provided care, at least on a full-time basis. Families may opt for professionally provided care, which includes working with in-home caregivers, adult day eldercare, independent living, assisted living, and dementia care. There is also a concept known as "continuum of care," sometimes called a Life Plan Community, which offers multiple stages of care from independent and assisted living to accommodating the progression of any care need, including dementia.

No one approach is right for every situation. For years, I have seen hundreds of examples of the progression of a person's dementia. I have learned that a person with dementia will need different levels of support before his or her journey is complete. Arrangements for eldercare support have different choices with pros and cons. Avandell will bring people a beneficial and pleasant environment that stands apart from traditional and rather regimented care model. The Avandell philosophy meets people where they are and gives them every opportunity to live a normalized lifestyle with due kindness and a well-trained, flexible staff.

IN-HOME SUPPORT

We see families caring for their elders in one of two ways. The older person can remain in his or her home where family members provide assistance. Alternatively, the elder moves in with a family member, who is typically an adult child. In either case, we frequently see in-home professional health workers coming in to supplement the support from family members. For example, professional elder care support is utilized during the workday or late at night, when family members are not available.

One issue that can happen with in-home support is having to depend on household employees who have neither the experience nor the desire to be involved with helping an elderly person as their care needs grow more complicated. It's "not their job." Helping an older person may feel too intense for housekeepers or live-in nannies taking care of babies. It is too much. Cleaning people may find themselves being asked to help with managing a strict medication schedule because they are already being paid. Some may be tasked to assist a person with dementia to the bathroom. Domestic employees are told to help with the person's hygiene and might have to clean up in the bathroom.

Often, the employee truly wants to be helpful but doesn't understand the facets of this extra part of their job. They are probably not as proactive as a family member might be. It is unrealistic to ask them to know what and how to share any important health or behavior information with the family. Adding extra job requirements for domestic employees can lead to anger or resentment. Unfortunately, asking them to do more may give them a good reason to quit due to new and unexpected eldercare chores they don't want.

With this in mind, household maintenance is key to helping the spouse or an adult child. Having a dedicated person working in the house to take care of laundry and cleaning is essential, especially if a spouse or adult child needs and wants to focus on helping a person with dementia.

For these reasons, it is usually best to hire a dedicated person for either the house or the elder without overlap. The Petersons hired Maria, the college student, to keep their mother company during the day. More often, the person caring for the loved one is a certified home health aide, or a companion. A person with this sort of training and job experience will know how to handle critical tasks like administering medications or speaking with doctors. In some cases, their services can be reimbursable through insurance.

Now comes the subject of agencies. There are a number of advantages to hiring an in-home worker from an agency versus doing the hiring yourself, which involves advertising and conducting background checks. If hiring in-home help yourself, you can have potential legal liability exposure. An agency usually will have professional liability insurance and manage paperwork. They will screen applicants and take care of arrangements such as help for day or night supervision. The agency can send someone in when a worker is sick and can't show up. On the downside, agencies may be very expensive. They may also be less flexible about what their staff will do in the home. An aspect of care that may not be discussed is the chemistry between the worker and the person with dementia.

It's worth clarifying the difference between "home care" and "home health care." Families and people with dementia generally need help with bathing and dressing, cooking, transportation to medical appointments etc. While people tend to use the terms interchangeably, they are not at all the same thing. Both terms refer to care in the home, but "home care" typically means an aide helping with activities of daily living, or a companion for engagement and socialization. Home care does not require nursing skills or medical expertise and does not need to be ordered by a physician.

Home health care, in contrast, means personnel in the home who have medical training and whose services are generally ordered by a physician. Home health care employees can help with checking a person's vital signs and respiration, and dealing with medical equipment, prosthetics or therapeutic treatments. As you can imagine, home health care staff has a greater cost, and for good reason. It may be inappropriate to overlap home health care with other services, such as housekeeping or maintenance.

ADULT DAY CARE

Adult day care, as the name suggests, is senior day care dedicated to older adults. People can thrive being a part of a community with interaction and activities that are part of a person's experience. This engagement might have been a good choice for Thomas Miller or Kathleen Peterson, though their families didn't pursue it.

At Avandell, we see how important it is to continue what people love to make them feel important and more like themselves. We are dedicated to keeping people as active as possible and will try to give them many alternatives to always watching TV. An older person is at risk of feeling isolated, even if they have people helping them at home. Many of the ideas that went into the Avandell concept were developed in our independent living communities—just modified to be suitable for people with dementia. We encourage and respect their independence and community access to things they love and are used to.

Families are able to choose from a range of adult day care models. All involve providing seniors with supervision and care in a structured, safe setting during the day. They usually operate on weekdays. Some adult day care facilities offer healthcare or support for dementia. This is a great option for people who can live at home but are not safe to be left home alone.

INDEPENDENT LIVING

Independent living provides for older people living on their own in houses or apartments. Some may be on a "55 and older" property or may have decided to transition to a senior living community that provides more assistance. A devoted neighborhood setting may have a putting green, aqua aerobics, and a bridge club. There are lots of social activities and professional support. The community will provide transportation.

For example, at UMC at Bristol Glen, residents have full access to a wellness and fitness center, a salon for hair and nails, and a place for spiritual services. There is a library, a social hall, and all sorts of activities. Residents can also choose from our dining options. The great thing about independent living is that people can enjoy their lives even if they choose to no longer drive, though many still keep their cars.

ASSISTED LIVING

As the aging process continues, and the progression of dementia affects an older person's ability to function independently, they or their families may opt for assisted living with a built-in plan to transition to more involved care as time goes by. This is a conversation we try to have early in the process.

There are a range of assisted living scenarios. Some are more institutional, almost hospital-like, while others are essentially apartment buildings with dedicated levels for a person's medical status. The benefit is that older people are now living in close proximity to trained staff who help with the full range of daily living activities.

Assisted living would also have been a good, early choice for the Millers and the Petersons. It might have provided a transition from the stress of home-based care before their family situations reached the point of crisis. Assisted living staff could have supported Thomas or Kathleen with medication management, meals, bathing, dressing, housekeeping, and transportation.

Both assisted living and memory care are residences offering twenty-four-hour supervision along with personal care assistance, meals, social activities, and various other amenities. We often work with families that are trying to make a decision between dedicated assisted living or memory care. The best approach is to work with a community that offers both or can "step a person from assisted living into memory care" if and when the choice becomes necessary. There often is an overlap and we keep channels open with families and loved ones to communicate what is happening so that the person is in the best place for their needs. Memory care is only for people with a number of different types of dementia whose lives are directly affected by the memory issues, although Alzheimer's Disease is the medical term that most people are used to hearing about.

SKILLED NURSING

If an older person needs around-the-clock nursing care, a skilled nursing facility (SNF) or "nursing home" is the best option. The supervising staff at a SNF will be licensed health professionals, including registered nurses (RNs), licensed practical nurses (LPNs), and nurses' aides. The residents' rooms are usually not private, as staff will come and go to care for the residents.

There are two types of nursing homes: long-term care and sub-acute skilled care. UMC developed a system to identify and develop a multidisciplinary team of professionals who exhibit the potential, skills, and desire to serve the elderly population and help them thrive in every facility for any level of care.

A long-term care facility has healthcare resources available on-site. Skilled care facilities are staffed by RNs and include staff with professional specialties, such as speech therapists, physical therapists, and occupational therapists. Sub-acute care is the most comprehensive, with a medical staff to manage medical treatments.

The challenge in a skilled nursing setting is to balance the delivery of outstanding healthcare with a plan for every resident's independence and dignity. An older person with health issues may have few cognitive problems. They are probably fully aware of what is happening to their health. It is difficult to come to terms with accepting human frailty. Our staff provides a great deal of compassion. On a daily basis, we encourage social interaction for residents to have as full a life as possible. Our approach involves offering activities and community participation to stimulate the mind and diminish the feeling of isolation. The joy of belonging is known to increase endorphins, promoting an incredibly helpful sense of well-being for people in elder care. UMC is dedicated to the benefits that result from the time and effort spent focused on a resident's mental and physical health.

MEMORY CARE

The term "memory care" refers to a spectrum of approaches that support people with dementia. I will go into this subject in more detail in the next chapter. Memory care is probably the best fit for Thomas and Kathleen, who are experiencing dementia. They need a living environment that is set up for them. Their families need to find the best fit within the different choices available.

Daily structure and activity are two of the most important elements of an effective memory care program. They may be periodically confused and disoriented, so keeping daily lives as normal as possible helps a great deal with their quality of life. Engaging people in activities is also very important. Even if a person's cognitive abilities have dropped off, their minds are still active—more active than you might imagine.

Let me add here that many senior communities utilize a strategy to change up whatever activity people with dementia are doing every twenty minutes based on their shortened attention spans. This is a strategy of distraction to avoid negative behaviors. UMC, by contrast, knows the residents well enough to engage them in meaningful things they like to do.

Memory care often has a higher staff to resident ratio. The difference in staffing ratios means that residents generally receive more support and attention. Memory care staff are trained to handle issues related to the person's changing cognitive, behavioral, emotional, and physical needs. The dedicated memory care communities also tend to have greater safety and security with more control and safety regarding restrictions on movement and access.

UMC is proud of our approach to the fundamental principles of Tapestries Memory Care. The people who come to live at UMC are welcomed with care and concern. Truly, what sets us apart from other elder care organizations is that upon accepting and receiving a new resident, the staff and families dedicate time to compiling a great deal of information about the person to make sure that their daily lives, the lives they are used to living, hardly change. How they lived before is how they will live at UMC.

Apart from adjusting to their new residence, a person is given free rein within the safe confines of the Tapestries neighborhood and encouraged to do what they would have done throughout their lives—on their own schedule. This independence and autonomy of life is honored. Staff will engage with residents and help them experience the fulfillment of each day. Employees who work at UMC are trained to provide assistance where needed, yet their training is to, first, be sensitive to stepping aside to allow as much independence as possible.

CONTINUING CARE RETIREMENT COMMUNITY (CCRC)

A CCRC is one that offers residents the widest possible range of options. We operate several sorts of these communities. Choices usually include independent living, assisted living, skilled nursing, and memory care. In some cases, they may even be connected to "active senior living" communities that are simply those "55+" housing developments or condo complexes designed with older people in mind before transitioning to actual senior care living.

The advantage of the continuum of care approach is that people can move in before serious issues related to aging set in. Then as their needs change, people can move into another part of a community offering different levels of services, such as assisted living.

In a full CCRC, there are type A, B, or C contracts. Type A is all-inclusive, and Type C is an a la carte option where, for example, the dining program may have various options from which a person can choose. Type B is a combination of Type A and C.

A continuum of care community is a good fit for couples where each partner is at a different stage of the aging process. They are in a safe, logical environment that can anticipate the progression of memory and physical conditions.

You can see that a continuum of care community might be a good option for Judith and Thomas depending on where they are in their aging journey. Thomas may be best suited for memory care. Someone like Kathleen might benefit from assisted living. In some assisted communities, people might be able to live together with their respective partners, with the person experiencing a decline in memory receiving specialized attention for dementia.

These are the main choices for helping a loved one receive support for aging and dementia. My intention in sharing this overview with you is to set the stage for understanding what can go right or wrong. You will have a good frame of reference for learning more about what has worked before and how Avandell is different and ideal for people with dementia.

CHAPTER 6

WHAT IS WORKING WELL IN THE CURRENT MODEL, AND WHAT COULD BE BETTER

In the Bible, the prophet Ezekiel, who is not happy with how the Israelites are treating their fellow man, says, "You eat the fat, you clothe yourselves with the wool, you slaughter the fat ones, but you do not feed the sheep. The weak you have not strengthened, the sick you have not healed, the injured you have not bound up, the strayed you have not brought back, the lost you have not sought, and with force and harshness, you have ruled them" (Ezekiel 34:3–4).

This is a significant lesson as it addresses how those of us at UMC go beyond the golden rule. We are dedicated to using everything in our community to truly strengthen the weak and heal the sick. We care. That is where we start—with caring and helping.

UMC and its staff agree on a moral and ethical code, an innate philosophy to make another person's life better if it is within our purview. We are *"committed to communicate."* People depend on us, and we take our responsibilities to heart every day. The UMC culture informs our entire approach to supporting families and the people they love as they travel on their journey with dementia.

Keeping our primary purpose in mind, as we have reviewed the major support options in the previous chapter, let's focus on memory care. There are many initial facets and choices of care that encompass ways to support seniors, which then expand to a wide range of approaches to memory care and the many different levels of quality and service.

Cost is certainly a factor, with less expensive facilities providing fewer services. In my career, I have repeatedly found that there is not always a connection between cost of care and quality. It depends on the institution, staff, and business philosophy. Yes, eldercare is a business, but virtually every organization I've known in the industry is not solely motivated by profit.

Organizations deliver memory care differently. In this chapter, we will take a look at how the predominant, current model works. We will explore some of the things that are working well and some that could be better. Most families don't know much about elder care until they need help. The goal of this chapter is to help people understand some of the challenges facilities and caregivers face and clarify why UMC has developed our Tapestries approach to supporting people with dementia. Tapestries has been the touchstone and inspiration that led us to visit De Hogeweyk™, giving UMC the beginning of our vision of the Avandell concept.

UNDERSTANDING MEMORY CARE

UMC currently delivers a traditional, clinical model of care, and, in addition to the traditional services, UMC has also expanded their approach. There is a distinction between skilled care (under skilled care regulations), assisted living, and memory care (under AL regulations). UMC continues to move away from previous models of care based on clinical evidence and overwhelming success in our approach to managing care for people who come to live with us in any of our communities. UMC does things differently and is constantly mindful of improving care and finding ways for residents to live their best lives.

The term "memory care" was developed because the world needed a description of how we help people with dementia in a residential setting. Memory care, in our vocabulary, refers to different types of approaches available to those affected by symptoms of dementia.

Memory care may be a dedicated floor in a nursing home and is intended to be a safe and structured environment. It offers people set routines. A philosophy of mindful care and a regular schedule based on a resident's personal rhythm have proven to considerably lower stress for people with dementia, as well as for staff who are not obligated to force a resident into a new institutional timetable for waking, eating, etc.

Assisted living offers staff that helps with things like meal service, escorting residents to activities, and assisting with personal care tasks. Memory care is different. The staff in this setting is usually trained to help with unique dementia issues that come up at all times of the day or night, whether the resident is affected by Alzheimer's or another type of dementia.

Memory care is an "assisted living facility—plus." The staff is tasked to check in with residents more frequently than they would in assisted living, where residents can generally be expected to manage their time and activities. Memory care provides extra structure and support to help people navigate their days and nights. This includes making sure that residents are eating and moving to whatever activity or process is next. People with dementia may wander, so many memory care units are locked. Entrances are accessible only by a coded keypad, with an intercom for visitors. Alarmed doors and elevators are similarly equipped with security and access codes.

Alleviating boredom is one of memory care's goals. People with dementia who are not adequately stimulated become bored, which can result in a myriad of responses such as anxiety, restlessness, and wandering off. Instead, with well-thought-out activities and diligent staff, residents can feel engaged and productive. Activities in the memory care setting are designed to support cognitive function and keep people engaged. They are meant to be fun, creative, and interactive if possible.

One of the foundational concepts in memory care is that a person with dementia will retain more of the person he or she was than we might imagine. It depends on the individual and at what stage medical professionals made a definitive diagnosis. Even if we don't see Professor Thomas Miller or Kathleen Peterson we once knew, they are still present on the inside.

Their difficulties in trying to communicate can be frustrating to them. It takes too much effort to explain themselves, or they are simply incapable of expressing what's on their mind in a way that others will understand. When people realize that they are not able to respond as they used to, frustration and fatigue can set in. We may see a person acting out in certain ways, maybe banging a cup or moaning when they stumble on their words or cannot communicate. For people with dementia, there often is a sense of giving up when the mind refuses to cooperate.

Anger or depression can affect their desire to feel inspired, have a sense of accomplishment, or even just to have a good time. This is where the staff at UMC shines because we are able to find something to make a resident's day better. We specialize in getting to know them and showing understanding, kindness, and community.

There are various ways to keep active and keep moving. Think about the cliché saying of Newton's First Law, "an object in motion stays in motion," or the similar "if you don't use it, you lose it." They are clichés for a reason. UMC researched the best options available for residents to stay active and happy. Sports and other physical activities like throwing a beanbag or passing batons back and forth may be part of the experience.

Studies find that fragrances are a part of long-term memory and residents may experience joy and increase their levels of energy taking in the wonderful scents of chicken soup, freshly baked cookies, and bread and apple pie fresh out of the oven. People remember and speak about childhood memories in great detail even when they cannot remember what happened during the last thirty seconds.

Some people with dementia may enjoy activities that entail using their hands. We offer cooking, music, art, various hobbies, and games and have found incredible value in certain tactile experiences like folding pieces of cloth.

Almost all of the established approaches to memory care include music, often with movement and dance. Yes, people can dance in their chairs and can be moved around in time to the music in wheelchairs. Anything to find joy in the sound! Music reaches a part of the brain associated with memory. Listening to and performing music that was part of one's past reactivates areas of the brain associated with emotion, speech, reasoning, and reward. There is incredible value in recognition of the fact that music from a person's life experience has created indelible memories. We are never surprised to hear people sing every word of a song they've known for sixty years.

Music and dance help people with dementia make positive connections. Susan Peterson said that her mother loved music. Any memory care residence where she might go would have to have music as an activity. UMC offers a lot of music therapy options. We like to invite children's groups to visit. They will sing and perform, and residents completely light up.

People with dementia can socialize, too. The value of relating to others is important, so company and interaction is essential. It may not look the way it used to, but it is definitely happening. For instance, Thomas has the desire to speak to people when he meets them. Even if others have trouble understanding what he is saying, they also will benefit from the attention of someone wanting to engage with them.

To bring interest and energy to a person's day, activities might include things like doing jigsaw or simple wood block puzzles. We provide sensory boxes with objects that have different textures and surfaces. Looking at photo albums and familiar objects can be wonderful and lead to moments of happiness and peace. We have residents who cannot really read anymore, but they love to hold and look through a newspaper. Reading the paper was something they did every day, so the familiarity of the action was reassuring. We recognize the important role of familiar objects and activities have in making people feel comfortable.

In some of our communities, we may show people old-fashioned things like a rotary telephone or a typewriter, which are familiar objects from their younger years. Nostalgia is comforting and prompts happiness and well-being. Art therapy, whether painting, crafts, weaving or collages, is a favorite.

One of the most popular events is when residents either take a field trip to a petting zoo or we bring in pets for a day of pet therapy. All residents, with or without dementia, light up when a Golden Retriever comes to visit.

All of this information is being reimagined at Avandell. People will have an opportunity to be out and about in a normal rhythm of living. Instead of experiencing life in a nursing home setting, people will be free to walk around their village, and staff will be able to direct them to recreational activities, but only if it fits with what a person wants to do at that moment.

THE BASICS

There are specific laws that were put in place that govern nursing homes and assisted living compliance and operations. These laws vary by state, but in general, nursing homes must meet established minimum requirements of care. For example, there is a mandate for nursing home residents to be fed three meals per day plus necessary supplemental nutrition, with the understanding that the senior is receiving food that meets FDA requirements. The resident's personal medical team would adjust their diets based on the individual's needs. He or she must be given assistance in getting to the bathroom, with hygiene help, as well as being regularly showered or bathed.

Some states may even stipulate the amount of time that staff spends with each resident. These laws will usually define requirements for a staff-to-resident ratio.

A personal, written service plan is required for all residents of any memory care facility. A service plan is written to spell out the non-clinical approaches staff will take with an individual. At a minimum, a service plan should incorporate necessities, including assistance with getting dressed, eating and using the toilet. These traditional plans cover dietary requirements and restrictions, including schedules for waking up and going to sleep.

A personalized service plan is helpful, but realities of facility design and staffing, along with policies, can get in the way. This is because it is easier for facilities to have all residents do the same things at the same time, such as a 5:30 dinner seating for everyone. The current paradigm requires that when a resident moves in, they need to adjust their daily routine to the rhythm of the institution.

Traditional facility operations are built around the rhythm of the institution. This is something we are on track to change with Avandell.

At UMC, our goal is that the institution will adjust its routine to the rhythm of the residents. **My mantra is that "nothing should change when a resident moves into a UMC community except their address."** This is for all of the various levels of housing and care UMC provides. This needs to be the standard across the board in the future for all housing.

Two further basic, mostly related, requirements to be aware of in memory care are risk mitigation and arrangements with healthcare facilities. Elderly people with dementia are at a greater risk for health problems and accidents. We have to take precautions to avoid residents getting injured or sick. Such risk management steps should be part of the service plan, as well as part of general policy. For instance, we may have floors mopped at night, when most residents are in bed, to avoid people slipping and falling.

It seems that there is a consensus that there will always be falls. You will see in the following chapter that a new culture of caring for the elderly was in place with Tapestries resulting in optimal care at Avandell. By being proactive, we look at challenges that affect individual residents and plan situations in advance to remove dangers or obstacles.

By understanding how things happen, we adjust to what a resident needs, not the other way around. We do our best to mindfully eliminate situations that might lead to accidents. It is only in knowing and taking the time to look at, assess, and understand a resident's day-to-day (and evening) patterns that we can adjust a living situation to make things safer and more comfortable.

There are ongoing relationships with nearby hospitals, primary health physicians, and geriatric specialists, including psychiatric experts. Doctors make house calls to visit residents in our communities.

We are trained to anticipate critical health issues that arise with older people, such as chest pains or symptoms of a stroke. We follow guidelines used by the National Stroke and American Heart Associations, which means watching out for facial drooping, arm weakness, speech difficulties and time; FAST is the acronym the association uses. Everyone is trained in symptom awareness, and we have defibrillators in all communities.

ISSUES THAT ARISE IN MEMORY CARE

Our industry is always adding to skills and practices to improve dementia care. That dedication is one of the main reasons we have developed the Avandell initiative. It is essential to be open to growth and change because improved care comes from understanding what can be done better and then taking the necessary action for a safer and happier community.

Problems are inevitable, however, even in a well-run facility. How we respond depends on regulation and organization policy and procedure. Unfortunately, there can be serious issues. We've all seen a variety of horrible headlines, such as a March 2021 NBC article titled *America now knows that nursing homes are broken. Does anyone care enough to fix them?* following the Covid-19 lockdowns and nursing home outbreaks.

Specifically, in my view, what is essential in a memory care environment is education and training. The staff that I work with is well-equipped to use focused skills they learned from UMC to deliver the best care. Staff sees residents every day and are the ones to recognize and understand that something is not working. Staff members should be able to bring up issues with their teams or supervisors. They should be supported in addressing certain core resident needs.

We want people with dementia to have a positive experience in our memory care communities. To facilitate this, Avandell sees the opportunity to be better, provide the best care and shorten the "what-can-go-wrong" list. That is our philosophy. We want to change the perception and the experience for residents and families. Avandell and Tapestries aim to be the paradigm, informing the leaders in the next generation of compassionate care for older adults with dementia.

AGITATION

Consider the problem of agitation. Statistics show that 20% of people with dementia have behavioral disturbances. Depending on the person, this may manifest as stubbornness or irritable rigidity. It can also mean screaming and yelling or even physical violence. In general, it is human nature to be agitated about something, at some point—dementia or not.

What is causing this agitation? If a person cannot express themselves in words, it is our job to figure it out. Our staff knows the residents well enough to do what we call "road mapping" the distress. Most importantly, they are empowered to take action to bring relief to the residents.

This is a question that has been an issue for nursing home staff members, management, and residents who live with someone who yells out and is obviously not comfortable. In an old way of doing things, if it is determined that a person's diagnosis, including dementia, still leads them to continually shout or moan, an expert geriatric psychiatrist and perhaps a different facility would be considered. Unfortunately, this is still practiced in many places.

We have concrete knowledge that most of the time when a person with dementia becomes agitated, it is because he or she is being deprived of autonomy or they are in pain. This comes back to the idea of the person without dementia still being present in the body of a person with dementia. As a UMC medical expert shares, "Sometimes it is as simple as two Tylenol." I promise you our staff will try to figure out what is causing a person's stress. Staff will inform and escalate pressing concerns to supervisors and management.

Professor Miller was accustomed to being respected and shown deference. He was also used to getting his way. Waking Professor Miller up at five am to change his incontinence garment or rushing to move him unclothed into a shower stall is not his thing. It's not anybody's thing, and why would it be? The problem is that Professor Miller can no longer communicate his wants and needs, yet deep down, he knows what he does not like, which is a violation of his preferred sense of privacy. He was angry to be completely unclothed in front of people he didn't know. Hence, agitation.

When staff and families of residents have discussions it turns out that the families are more upset than their relative or loved one about transitioning to using an incontinence garment. We know that the residents almost always accept wearing the garment, whether overnight, due to incontinence, or not being able to move quickly enough to a toilet. Families don't like the idea of doing so but this takes so much pressure off of everyone.

A person with dementia may show anger or be upset when they are told the word "no" too often. "No, you can't watch the TV channel you want. No, you can't go outside. No, you can't stand up and walk around. No, you can't eat lunch now," etc. For each of these "nos," there is usually a logical policy or staff determination. At UMC, we work hard to say "yes" more often than "no," because we mindfully manage a person's environment and get to know who they are and what they need. Issues that cause people to be upset are often so small. We absolutely have to investigate and get to the root of the problem. It is the only way to manage things, especially long-term.

In traditional facilities, not addressing obvious discomfort and stress can cause more agitation and a cascade of consequences. He or she may be intentionally isolated—separated from other residents or not allowed to take part in activities. This may make the problem worse, even though not including the person in the general resident population is understandable.

MEDICATIONS

Agitation can lead to a request to prescribe medication for the person with dementia. This is a contentious issue, often an easy fix, which can turn out to be unnecessary and harmful to the resident. These drugs, called chemical restraints, are not only unnecessary, but can be harmful. Medications meant to calm or diffuse the situation of an agitated resident can cause unwanted side effects, falls, and/or premature death. Most psychotropic medications have a black box warning for people with dementia, meaning that the side effects are terrible.

One of the doctors we work with described his process of assessment. He begins with a thorough look at the behavior he's being asked to examine. "I get called in, usually by the staff, who say, 'we think that this person definitely needs to be medicated.' When the resident is harassing staff or is really out of control, I understand that we certainly need to do something."

The doctor continued, "I came in to consult for a situation where a resident was biting the nurses. This is where I take the time to ask a lot of questions because we all really have to figure out what's going on. For example, if a resident has been moved from one floor to another and is presenting with a problematic state of agitation, the solution might point to not seeing his regular dinner table or activity companions. The move has made him agitated. That is most likely not a situation where medication is going to be the right approach."

In the eldercare environment, for every type of facility, the issue of medicating to placate needs to be discussed. The doctor added, "I will again underscore that it is so important to find actual issues affecting patients. I agree that in our industry, the way people with dementia are medicated leaves much room for improvement."

Here is the other side of "meaning well without enough information." The doctor explained, "Medication requests often come from family members. They call and say, 'My mother is unhappy. I think she needs anti-depressants.' Medication may or may not be indicated in that situation."

The geriatric psychiatrist needs to know how to tease out what is genuine depression from situational, temporary mood changes. In some cases, an anxious family member will say, "do something," when they cannot fix things. A skilled geriatric psychiatrist should be able to interpret the symptoms and prescribe effectively.

People with dementia can definitely become depressed or anxious, though. That is real, and medication may be the correct solution in these cases. Remember, on the inside, the person is still there. We welcome families to share their thoughts. Judith Miller told us that occasionally when her husband worked, he experienced anxiety attacks. This sort of information would really help us during the initial interview. If Thomas's anxiety resurfaced, we would be ready, understanding that he would not be able to explain things himself.

In some cases, a physician will determine that sedating drugs are necessary. A respected geriatric psychiatrist shared with me, "The challenge is to use them only when necessary and avoid over-using them."

UMC staff has been thoroughly trained in policies and practices to minimize over-medicating residents. Again, this is an example of eliminating issues by not letting there be a problem in the first place by getting to know the residents.

Avandell's goal is to create an environment where the phrase "he needs to be medicated" is heard less often. Tapestries, as mentioned in the Introduction, has been successful in this regard, and the experience influenced Avandell. We are prepared to bring the best of care, and practices and procedures in place to, as Rabbi Jeff Sirkman said, "meet people where they are."

SHIFT HANDOFFS

When one shift ends and another starts, staff members have to share important information, such as the notes and instructions about each resident. Perhaps someone needs a later dinner because he had a medical procedure that overlapped with his dinner time. This might seem minor, but many times I've seen a person with dementia who is hungry yet cannot express what's on his mind. Perhaps a later lunch or snacks to bring along with instructions for the aide or person accompanying the resident may help. Otherwise, the resident may become agitated. This is the proactive thinking built into UMC's standard of care. Multiply the idea of this specific instance by one hundred, and you can see the reality of essential shift change communications every day, seven days a week.

Memory care is a round-the-clock concern, so handoffs between shifts are critical for ensuring a good experience for residents. There are three vital ingredients for making this work. Staff members must be trained and diligent. Management needs to be a partner, not a judge, so that staff feels comfortable sharing the good moments and any concerns. Then, we look for employees who exhibit a certain instinct and sense of empathy during the interview process.

We will recognize a successful candidate who wants to join UMC when the potential associate shows enthusiasm for helping people with dementia. UMC requires applicants to be perceptive and proactive. Communication is encouraged. It is usually very clear when applicants are eager to join us. They are the right people for a job because they tell us that this is their calling—they were meant to help these older residents continue to have good lives in their new home.

We want staff who share our philosophy of helping people enjoy their fullest possible lives. Being able to articulate events of the day and inform the next shift is essential. We want people on staff who are problem solvers. We find that these traits of responsible excellence create a work culture for staff to thrive and be happy in their careers.

PROBLEMATIC BUT PERSISTENT PRACTICES

As people with dementia enter a memory care environment, they will have an adjustment period in adapting to a new setting. Moving anywhere can be disorienting, especially when coupled with new routines and unfamiliar people. As we have said, this can manifest as agitation and other behaviors that are uncomfortable for the person with dementia and the staff.

So, what can be done about obvious discontent? The traditional approach was to physically restrain the person's arms or their body so they would not get up and be a danger to themselves or others. The image of elderly, confused people being restrained can upset everyone. This is why the industry has gone to great lengths to stop this practice.

If the level of agitation escalates, we will send a resident out to the hospital or provide one-on-one care until we are able to send them out for medical treatment.

I'm not excusing the practice of restraint here. My point is that policy is put in place for the safety of residents and staff. Facilities often follow standard operating procedures, such as staffing ratios and program design.

It is frustrating for everyone involved when a person with dementia is having a hard time. Certainly, the resident is unhappy and is struggling to somehow communicate in the only ways they can. It's hard on staff and supervisors, partly because it's frustrating to figure out how to calm down a person who cannot articulate or even point to a body part that might hurt.

It can sometimes be an incredible challenge to take care of everyone. We prioritize residents' needs over everything else. This is one of the key elements of the UMC household model and person-centered care. There are many staff responsibilities, and UMC takes its legal obligation and commitment to the best care very seriously. Residents come first.

We monitor our residents and know ahead of time when they may need something because we've done a detailed resident profile and have information about what they like and what their lives were like before joining us. We have information about their schedules in their homes. The resident profile has been key and informs the staff on the preferences of the resident. We keep track of one thing that may impact another and can avoid episodes if we know what might happen if we are not vigilant.

UMC devotes a lot of time to very important actions, such as keeping the person's room as familiar as possible. Avandell encourages "bringing an old lamp the person is familiar with and knows how to turn on." We ask families to bring their loved one's special, comfortable chair, the sheets they are used to sleeping on and any pictures that make their new home feel like home to them. They may have an old worn-out radio that can be turned on without assistance because it is their radio.

It takes a minute to explain to families that the newest, helpful technology to hit the market may not actually be helpful for their loved one. Families mean well by giving residents things to make life easier. However, introducing something that they had not learned about and used before can truly confuse and upset them. We say, "let them have their old things," because the transition is less jarring and allows them to feel at home.

We learn about a person's daily rhythm; for example, the time they get out of bed and what they eat for breakfast. An individual's daily routine is paramount and unique to them. We honor that.

I'll emphasize it again; UMC hopes that when a new resident enters one of our communities, the only thing that changes is their address.

THE STAFF-FACING PARADIGM AND THE NEED FOR CHANGE

Many of the most serious issues affecting memory care come down to this: for any given policy or practice, whom is it intended to benefit? Most policies and practices today are "staff-facing." They were devised by management and staff from their professional point of view, for the institutional efficiency. For example, if breakfast is from 7–8:30 a.m., then all residents eat breakfast during that time, and there is no flexibility built-in, except for certain residents who will receive a tray in their rooms or those who must be hand fed for resident's specific medical reasons.

In contrast, a "resident-facing" paradigm is geared to the needs of the resident first and the staff second. Under this approach, if the resident wakes up late, then he should get breakfast without any discussions. This is obviously far, far easier said than done. Deciding on this sort of policy takes planning, staff input, flexibility, and rethinking many aspects of memory care.

Having a staff-facing paradigm does not automatically mean that the quality of life of residents is low. My point is that a resident-facing paradigm can deliver much better outcomes. Tapestries is built on the idea of resident-facing policies and practices, which are instilled into the design of Avandell. Tapestries is all about meeting people where they are and fitting into the schedules they lived before joining us—as best as possible.

The model is based on what the resident wants and how the staff and community can help them be comfortable. Because our professional staff knows ahead of time, or quickly learns what suits a resident, we can accommodate the person without stressing out the staff or causing problems for other residents. It is achievable when we prioritize gathering all possible information. There are fewer surprises, and the level of happiness shines.

PROACTIVE STRATEGIES

For a resident-facing policy to work, it has to be proactive, rather than reactive. Let me give you an example. Judith Miller said that her husband became difficult after they moved him from one room in the house to another. The new ground floor room was safer and larger. Thomas didn't have to deal with going up and down stairs. Most of the adjustment worked, but his mood became harder to handle. He started to wake up at two in the morning, making lots of noise that woke up the household.

I think I know what was happening, and it's the sort of subtle issue that can cause big problems if it's not anticipated. What was probably going on with Thomas is that his new room had more light in it. I asked Judith, and she confirmed this to me. His new ground-floor room did not have as much shade as his upstairs room. The tree branches outside would block the outside light upstairs. Downstairs he was woken up by streetlights.

As a result, his circadian rhythms became disrupted. Add to that the fact that Thomas's melatonin supplies were dropping. This is common for older people. Sleep can be hard to come by as we age. Thomas's internal clock was off, which affected everyone.

In a memory care neighborhood, we try to be proactive about this sort of thing. If someone is being moved to the other side of the building or to a room with a smaller window we try to think through what this might mean for their sleep patterns and general happiness. If we're paying attention and being proactive, we can avoid the difficulties that might otherwise arise. If they are comfortable, we might encourage residents to spend time in front of a sunny window or outside on a nice day. It's not that hard, once you've figured out what the issue is and taken proactive steps, to make it right.

We manage other sensory issues such as noise sensitivity and any number of factors that trouble people with dementia. We can address these variables and keep people healthy and comfortable with proven, proactive strategies.

We will go a lot deeper into proactive, resident-facing approaches to memory care as we discuss Tapestries in the next chapter.

CHAPTER 7
SEEKING A SOLUTION

Things are getting better. It's taken a while, but our approach to assisted living and memory care now puts UMC on the cusp of offering a groundbreaking dementia village. **Our intention in serving the geriatric population is to allow people to live the lives they love. We come from the perspective of positivity: "Saying yes more than no."**

Part of changing our standards and practices means dropping old school language. Now, we refer to "people living in households and communities" as opposed to "patients living in a unit" or "in the west wing of the nursing home." We're more "person-centric" rather than "patient-centric." The words we use to describe what we do and how we do it changed to reflect kindness, respect, humanity, and community. "Memory support" is now "memory care."

The positive change in care did not come from our trying to be *politically correct*. Our genuine philosophy and perception of what elder population support should look like completely respects the person who has come to live with us. Their individual humanity is recognized and embraced by the community.

Tapestries embodies these precepts. The Avandell concept is an extension of Tapestries, whose goal has been to be a lot less clinical and much more focused on normalcy and authentic living. UMC created this social model based on heavy research. Much of the elder care industry supporting seniors is beginning to adopt similar methods of serving their residents—validating UMC's leadership role in the industry.

THE FAMILIAL HOUSEHOLD

One of the foundations of Tapestries is the idea of a "familial household."

The idea is to have residents live in an environment that feels more like a house and less like an institution. If we create a culture that comes from a place of kindness, responsibility, and community, there is a much more positive beginning to our relationship with the person, their family, and loved ones. UMC aspires to treat residents like family. This is the best way to start.

Until we build our first Avandell location, we are in existing buildings in different parts of New Jersey. At The Shores, we have two "households" with fourteen residents each. In three other buildings, we have somewhere between twenty-one and twenty-three people. The neighborhoods are staffed with two aides for fourteen residents or three aides for the building with twenty-one people.

Tapestries, and its familial household approach, is partly about space and process, but our people are the ones who make it happen. To make the familial household work we had to cross-train our staff. We were one of the first organizations in the industry to undertake the huge challenge of moving employees away from having singular jobs. For example, we eliminated the Community Life (Activities) Department as a stand-alone entity within the Tapestries neighborhood. Now, all staff members have some involvement in activities. Formerly single-purpose certified nursing assistants have additional roles and are now responsible for dishes, laundry, and medications for the household.

We are putting the new paradigm into practice. All residents will see only one dedicated staff member for most of their care. It is incredibly helpful that people see that one staff person's face, to form a vital relationship with them during a shift.

This change was not intuitive, and to be honest, at first, it was a hard sell to staff. Requiring people to do dishes was the biggest "ask," and they were not happy with the expansion of their job descriptions. However, once the staff adjusted to a new routine, everyone began to understand why we were making the change and how it was positively affecting everyone's experience.

The shift in role expansion is part of the big picture of an atmosphere of putting the resident first. UMC gave staff ownership of the new cross-trained and cross-functional roles. The result? Less stress and longer employment tenures.

This was a welcome development. Some people only work in our industry, eldercare, for less than one year. They burn out working in other facilities that are staff-centric rather than resident-centric. This makes sense if you understand the stress of that sort of environment.

The cross-training and new roles inherent in Tapestries brought out the best in people. It gave people the insights they needed to stay with their jobs longer. At UMC we have expert staff that were born for this job and have thrived taking care of older people for many years. Caring for that many people takes a great deal of dedication and a special sort of person who chooses to work in an environment devoted to so many people in one place. Tapestries brought out this potential in people.

Once staff members understood why the new approach to roles worked, they got it, and it's been a success. We have continued to grow and expand everything—all of this a significant departure from the old nursing home model of people sitting in wheelchairs or in corners of rooms with little interaction and no joy.

The team effort of the Tapestries vision of memory care depended on vital staff from the UMC home office to help craft and work on the project. What UMC has done with Tapestries is add a layer and then another for all of us to work together serving those with dementia.

We have a great Corporate Director of Tapestries Initiatives, Pam Garofolo, an expert in dementia support who also oversees the Community Life cohort system-wide. Pam has the unofficial title of Dementia Care Specialist. She is immersed in resident engagement, often joking around with staff in such a very sweet way, that her title is "Director of puppies and kittens and everything non-clinical."

A day in our Tapestries households starts with something called "natural rising." We have agreed that we don't wake up our residents. Whenever a resident decides that they are going to get up and start their day, that same staff person whom they know will greet them.

The cross-trained employee will provide any assistance the resident needs. It's important to tell you that we encourage our residents to be independent, so staff will perform something more like guided care. We try not to do too much for them, so they experience autonomy and independence, basically the same life they've always lived, to keep their rhythm and schedule that they would have had at their homes before moving into our residences. You eat your breakfast whenever you wake up; it's just like in your house.

Then, that same aide will dispense medications. There are no universal set medication times. The medication is given at a time based on the needs of the resident and not the needs of the community, as was always the case in nursing homes that woke people up at 6:30 a.m. for meds and then had a set evening medication time for all residents.

PERSON-CENTRIC ENGAGEMENT

UMC goes out of its way to elevate the level of how we care about residents. Our term is "person-directed." The key to success is "know thy resident," and anticipating what an individual wants and desires, which increases the frequency and quality of engagement.

A perfect example from one of our Tapestries neighborhoods is the morning routine established by a group of male residents. They take their time getting to the dining room but end up gathering at the same table between 9 and 10 a.m. These gentlemen will sit down with their cups of coffee and newspapers, and staff will top them off every 15 minutes or so. Staff will never take them out of their men's newspaper ritual group for other activities because their schedule is indelible in their routines. Why would we disrupt them for what we think they should be doing?

They remind us of any group of guys, single, divorced, or widowed men, that you may see sitting at a diner for hours. Men of a certain era in this age group may or may not acknowledge each other with a nod of the head, rarely saying hello to each other. At breakfast they are each looking at their own copy of the newspaper, maybe not actually reading but still shaking their heads as though they are able to follow the news.

Thomas Miller found this group on his second day with us, or perhaps the group found him, but it was a perfect fit. He took his seat at the table, grabbed a newspaper, and nursed a cup of coffee for a good hour or two before going on to his next activity.

For these people, allowing them their customary life is what successful engagement looks like because we don't interfere. This is their happy place. UMC fosters and encourages those things that add value and joy to people's lives. Perhaps a good way to put it is that we respect and say yes as much as we can while helping people to live their lives as they always have—with the familiarity of what is normal to them. Again, part of our philosophy is that in the big picture, all that has changed is their address.

There are many residents who enjoy group activities. Sometimes we have people who do their own thing, such as ladies who want to be "helpers." Kathleen Peterson fit into this role. She is a resident, but her instinct is to care for others. She does what she thinks she should do, and we don't get in her way.

Helping keeps Kathleen on an even keel throughout the day. She always makes sure that she is the first person, besides staff, to say hello to new residents—almost adopting them so they will have an instant friend. Most of the time, Kathleen never remembers his or her name but tells everyone, "This is my nice friend," with a certain amount of pride.

There is a lovely woman who has always been "a cleaner." She is happiest when constantly wiping or tidying things. Once we realized what she was doing and why, we gave her a cleaning cloth. Every day she sets out on her mission to clean the same tables one hundred times. Her happy place is to contribute to her environment. We support her and help her express what makes her happy and keeps her occupied. Contributing by doing is her normal life. We say yes to continue giving her a reason to be a part of things in a way that is meaningful to her.

Person-centric engagement can yield some remarkable breakthroughs in resident experiences. This doesn't always happen, but as staff gets to know residents better, they sometimes gain some useful insights into what makes them tick—enabling them to bring joy and avoid upset. With Thomas Miller, attentive staff members noticed that he seemed to get agitated toward the end of mealtimes. We could not figure out what was going on with him.

Finally, having taken the time to get to know Judith and hear stories about her marriage to Thomas, the staff member connected the dots and realized that Thomas was accustomed to picking up the check when he took people out to dinner. For Thomas, the dining room was a group meal, sort of like a restaurant. So, he was waiting for the check, and he became nervous that someone else would take care of it.

Our people solved this problem by giving Thomas an expired credit card and telling him that he could pick up the check any time he felt like it. Well, guess what? Now, Thomas frequently takes that credit card out of his pocket at mealtimes and hands it to one of our staff members to settle the bill. He is no longer upset at mealtimes. This is the kind of win we see with Tapestries and person-centric engagement.

Another resident became agitated in the evenings. It was not at all clear what was bothering him, except the pattern was so distinct that we figured it had to be based on time of day. After speaking with his family, our staff learned that this gentleman spent many years working as a security guard at a hotel. It was his job to check that all the doors and windows were locked at the end of his shift.

Now, we ask this resident if he will help us check the doors and windows each night. He gets up and does exactly that—his old job, ensuring the building is secure. Then, when he no longer feels anxious about being derelict in his duties he is ready for bed.

These may seem like simplistic examples but unless the staff "know thy resident" they cannot connect the dots and reduce the resident's distress.

RESPECTING ROUTINES

Tapestries honors the people who come and live with us. They bring their routines with them. We endeavor to discern what a resident's daily pleasure is and then try to replicate it. Some people wake up at 6 a.m. or 11 a.m. We don't force anyone to eat or dress at a certain time. We'll ask them, "Do you want to wait for lunch, or do you want breakfast now?" There is a regular, structured "sitting down time" at noon, and people will either eat the prepared lunch or there may be an alternative—something we already know from experience with them, that will be part of their routine—whether cottage cheese, toast, and tea or an open turkey sandwich. We serve whatever the residents eat, and we always have the option of having finger foods or sandwich ingredients available if a resident is happier making their own sandwich. We always keep the kitchen available and open.

On the theme of always saying yes, we are mindful to constantly adapt and switch things up when necessary. Improvisation, switching things up, is one of the things that Tapestries instilled at UMC to boost our level of community care and normalizing life. The big theme is flexibility in what we do. The staff is prepared with regular training, and constant communication to adapt to a person's ability or wishes.

You see then that a schedule, now a looser term in an elder care setting, is based on the individual's needs and preferences. We offer some element of structure but a resident is free to not follow that structure. We learn about how they navigate the day and support them and their choices, keeping in mind their physical and mental health along with safety.

Consider Bill, someone who we learned was a professional drummer before he came to live with us. We had a cool drum kit for him once we learned about his past. He was a resident at UMC before he transitioned to Tapestries. The "old school model" led the staff to tell me he was up all night and "we need to do something about that." They wanted to try medicating him at night, along with keeping him engaged in activities during the day to tire him out because, "he was up all night, and it was a problem."

UMC was then just at the beginning of discussing a more practical social model, so the Tapestries Director said, "Let's try a different approach. Let's try and let him stay up." We did our research to find out why he had a completely different time clock. Well, the reason he was living the way he was living was because he had been a professional drummer playing in bands every night. Sometimes his day didn't start until nine oclock or, because he played jazz, even at midnight. In "those days," he got home around sunrise, after playing two or three sets, then always had a meal after a concert.

Bill also became friendly with the staff member from the 11 p.m. to 7 a.m. shift because he was awake and a bit lonely for company. We started letting him sleep until noon, and he was so much more comfortable getting up then. Some nurses had a difficult time adapting to this flexible schedule for Bill. The night nurse felt a responsibility and worried that he was sleeping through breakfast and might lose weight. He did lose a bit of weight, but we found a solution by offering him a third meal at night. If he had been out performing, he would have easily gone for a "breakfast as dinner" scenario. That is one of the things we did for him. We did not impose our timeline on his life.

UMC is all about life solutions. We gave him three meals whenever his body clock asked for them. Staff started making him sandwiches at 9 p.m. He was active all afternoon and had good energy, so they let him stay up at night until 3 a.m. He went to bed much happier, I would even say completely content. We didn't have to give him medications. The staff was happier, and the night staff person had someone to keep her company.

SUPPORTING FAMILIES

Supporting people's mental health and well-being is always front and center with Tapestries. Many of our staff have some background and training in mental health counseling, and we never know when we can put their skills to use. The value of being sensitive to emotional needs is especially important when dealing with families. We always say, "Our staff uses their skills every day communicating with families and fellow staff members." And yes, it is every day.

The idea of facing the future is a hot button that some people admit to avoiding (as did their parents), but now they are immersed in decision-making where so many feelings tend to appear. We validate family members and how they express their emotions. We try to release them from their fear and guilt. All of us do the best we can with the tools available. Depending on where families or partners are in the process of home care or considering our community, we help them take small steps to make changes or sometimes give specific direction if they are paralyzed with emotion. It really helps when we can bring joy and humor to what they are going through.

Sometimes there is a gift in the midst of the dementia experience, for example, when a woman started to call her daughter "mother." Our staff was able to explain to the adult daughter that her mother did not really think that she, her daughter, was actually her mother. Instead, the mother, our resident, was confused about what word to use to explain, "A woman who loves me more than anything." The daughter was then able to see that every time her mother with dementia called her "Mom," she was really being told, "Thank you for loving me."

Contributing to these moments and conversations are life changing and a privilege for the staff. These are the types of rewards in our profession that make it worth coming to work every day.

One of the most important things is to be neutral without judging when we find ourselves in any situation. During a tour, I had a conversation with a man I had just met that same day. He brought up the old reputation of nursing homes and abuse and wanted to know how having dementia puts people at risk for abuse.

I had not expected this question to come up then, but we talked about it. Many people think an abuser is just waiting to hurt someone and selects a person with dementia because the person cannot report it. The reality is much more complex. People with dementia can be very frustrating to those not trained in taking care of someone who has it. The person might be barraging those around them with repetitive questions, can be paranoid and, at a certain point, it is mostly impossible for the family member to reason with the resident.

Pam, the Corporate Director of Tapestries Initiatives, mentioned earlier, shared her experience with her father yelling at her mom for asking the same questions repeatedly, and her mom crying because she did not understand what she had done wrong. This was Pam's revelatory moment, which motivated her to ask for help. There is also the unexpected scenario when a family member might be trying to help a loved one and the person, more childlike than adult, will lash out and hit the person trying to help them. If someone hits you, without thinking, you may hit back out of sheer reflex, which is not acceptable. Under other circumstances, defending yourself would be a normal reaction. Think of how hard it must be to be angry and helpless simultaneously. It would be logical that neither the resident nor the family member had the intention of hitting the other.

The struggle to communicate can translate to struggling with everything. A family member does not have the context and training as would a dementia care professional with years of experience. The adult child can react to the person with dementia without having even a moment to get their bearings. Add in years of frustration or family history with the parent or partner that has built up until that moment and you have physical contact not meant to be abusive.

This is something that can happen. Our staff understands and does not judge anyone in these situations. Once a person has hit or pushed a loved one without realizing what was happening, it usually never happens again. At this point, we recommend getting some space. Maybe it is time for family members to go on vacation, take some time away from their loved one, or maybe consider a therapist.

We have a support group and encourage family members, friends, and partners to attend. Support groups are effective in helping to focus on the mental health of the family member.

Everyone reacts differently, but I understand how people deal with a part of life that no one ever expected. When caring for someone becomes too difficult, this might be a really good time to consider moving into a memory care community.

SUPPORTING STAFF MEMBERS

These issues are just as relevant for the staff. A daily, emotionally intense environment is not for everyone. Our dedicated Tapestries staff is carefully screened. They are beyond special and have a higher tolerance for unexpected behavior because they are ready for it. However, and this is important, staff rarely know they are on the verge of burnout and work fatigue.

“We maintain a strong sense of humor and and a work bond among colleagues that mirrors soldiers on the battlefield. Many people who are not in our shoes would just not understand. UMC supports us, which then helps us continue to do our best for our residents,” expressed Pam.

It is possible that some staff in very stressful work situations may experience PTSD or may accumulate levels of stress. This was an issue in traditional nursing homes for individuals who put in so many hours and had not realized the toll it can take. I have had many conversations with staff about not overdoing it. Pam suggests that perhaps they switch their present job assignments.

UMC took the time and opportunity with Tapestries to offer the best training and to implement how we gather essential information about individuals with dementia who come to live in our communities. We can avoid and get ahead of circumstances. UMC’s best practices are what set us apart from other memory care and elder care communities. Mental health for both residents and staff is a priority, and we work in a safe, comfortable, and transparent space with communication always encouraged and supported.

No one would ever imagine that some of our staff, friendly and engaged in public, may privately be introverted or shy. They are professionals and always rise to the occasion when families and other staff unburden issues or need assistance with problem-solving. Maybe people, whatever their role, just need someone to talk to. We are in the position of being polite and empathetic. On a daily basis we listen to concerns, major fears, guilt, and idiosyncrasies about family members’ own mortality. People want to tell us their stories. There are always so many feelings and so much that has been tucked away or not said as people live their lives.

Defining moments bring out a person’s reality and sometimes feelings that have been held back out of shame, fear, or uncertainty. They can pour out when we least expect it. Our professionals are equipped to listen. They are the best in the profession and provide excellent care and compassion.

We are immersed in the world of caring for others. Every day we have our radar up and are ready to meet daily challenges. Sometimes when speaking with families, first, we need to say, "I am sorry if I come across as blunt or too direct, but I suspect that is what you want," and they almost always want the truth.

Being a problem solver can be exhausting. People who work in dementia care need time to decompress and find some solitude to recover from giving their focused attention and energy to all of our residents. Unfortunately, when they leave work, staff members experience their friends and families being uncomfortable when they tell them about their days.

When people find out we work in dementia care, they express pity or tell us that it is nice of us to sacrifice ourselves for such a difficult job. It is important to find an outlet or peers who can more comfortably hear about our days for our own mental health.

This is a perfect example of what we've discussed in previous chapters. I find it sad that people are afraid of addressing dementia and aging until sometimes they are exhausted and appear on our doorstep, ready to move their parent or loved one into our community. The avoidance of what comes with aging is an issue that is so common, and a great percentage of people don't want to think about it. They don't want to talk about their fears and often will feel paralyzed. We'll look at this more in the next chapters.

Members of our staff had parents with dementia. It is very different being a professional caregiver and being a daughter or son of a parent with dementia. Family members think that if there is a dementia care professional in the family, they will take care of everything. On the other hand, when professionals talk to their families about moving the parent into care, the siblings resent someone being the expert. Sometimes you just can't win. The personal experience definitely helps a staff member and builds their professional capabilities.

One of our staff members told us, "My own kids know what I want and don't want as I age—or if I get sick. We talk all the time." As teenagers, they knew what a DNR (Do Not Resuscitate) was, and when the staff member wanted it to take effect.

"If you ask my kids what I want when I get dementia, they will tell you, 'We are going to put her in a dementia community, give her a clipboard, and tell her she works there.'"

THE MOVE IN

When families have their first tour of Tapestries, they visit the office of our Tapestries Director. She will interview them and ask about their loved one. If they mention words such as confused, we need to clarify what confused looks like and specifically means to them. Staff will give input to families and help them to understand whether what they are experiencing is typical or not. UMC professionals may make referrals to neurology, as a formal diagnosis of dementia is rare.

We have specific departments designated to transact finances and register the residents joining our community. We also ask them to complete a personal profile. If, through talking to a family, we decide the person is not a good fit, we'll talk about why.

Trust is vital to the relationship between UMC professionals and families. They are encouraged to be in touch with our Tapestries Director with any questions and are given suggestions to attend support groups, even if they do not choose UMC.

The move-in process is very emotional, and UMC does a lot of handholding through this. Staff are reminded to be patient with families if they are rude or controlling. An interesting observation is that it is extremely common for families to take out frustration on the staff. However, after a number of months, families and associates can become best friends and true partners in caregiving.

After two weeks, we schedule a care conference, which again includes a lot of counseling. This is the point where we often recommend a family vacation. We assure them that we can focus on the hard part, i.e. bathing and overall caregiving, and they can shift back to the fun part of interacting with their loved one, such as spending time and doing activities. From this point forward, there will be scheduled care conferences every six months, or as needed.

As this overview has reflected, Tapestries has positively impacted resident experiences at UMC. This chapter also revealed that getting an initiative of this scope off the ground is a huge project. It involved rethinking how we operate, how we train people, the roles people perform, and so much more. Tapestries represents a massive shift in the way we do dementia care. The investment of time and resources has been worth it on many levels, though. Everyone's experience improved. But also, Tapestries has put UMC in an excellent position to make Avandell a reality.

CHAPTER 8

AVANDELL: A NEW MODEL FOR DEMENTIA CARE

I hope you are enjoying a window into UMC with a view into how our devotion to finding new and better ways to serve people with dementia has led us to this momentous point as our team puts our plan into action. UMC and the Tapestries initiative guided dementia care on a special journey to develop Avandell, and I'd like to tell you more about how it will work.

As you've read, UMC has been part of the industry's evolution toward better modes of memory care. Our team worked with families and people with dementia for years. UMC stands out in developing some significant advances, resources and practices for interacting with residents and families who need dementia care.

As mentioned, Avandell is the next step in a departure from traditional care. The new transformational approach to dementia care provides a safe environment where people can live their lives without much change.

A memorable moment of inspiration for me came in the form of glass and bricks. I was in one of the UMC residences looking at a wall and wishing for the life of me that it could disappear. We really wanted to do more with that space and make it work better for the residents. Easier said than done. We just couldn't move the darn wall because it was structural and held up a big part of the building.

That's when it hit me. To take memory care to the next level we had to modify the physical environment. UMC needed to build a new space to provide the best environment to support the best care.

Of course, space isn't everything. You can have a marvelous space but offer mediocre care. However, with the right space, you have the freedom to become more people-centric. We want the people we work with and for to live the lives they love. For most people with dementia, a physical setting that resembles a hospital does not work well. It can feel stale and claustrophobic, even daunting and cold. The institutional feeling reminds people they are no longer in their homes. It says, "You are not living the life you love anymore—you are somewhere else, somewhere strange . . ."

AVANDELL: THE RHYTHM OF THE DAY

Avandell is a combination of several innovative concepts for dementia care. The enclosed village and the way it functions blends a new approach to optimal physical space that provides a more normal life for residents; with the best elements of our Tapestries program.

Avandell is built as an enclosed village with parks and special nature spaces where residents can experience butterflies, and flowers. It has lovely houses, streets, stores, and restaurants. Of course, it's not an actual village. Cars are not allowed and will not be able to drive through.

The space is secure, with no access for the residents to leave. However, inside the village, daily life is as normal as possible. That is UMC's goal. People live in their houses, go to the grocery store or post office, and have a community space to enjoy hobbies or meet new people—if they want to. The important thing is that when they move to Avandell, the only major change is their address.

Picture Avandell as an enclosed series of purpose-built buildings with outdoor spaces. People can walk around or socialize. It looks like an ordinary town. Imagine a type of outdoor shopping mall made to resemble a village square with a protected outer wall that is not obvious to people with dementia. The houses look out on the main street that leads to the main square.

Residents eat together, as friends or families would, in their seven-person houses, managed by a team of staff members.

Avandell's houses take our "familial home" model from Tapestries and applies it to a special, safe setting. With only seven people in each house, we've organized Avandell houses to look like a normal family setting in a neighborhood where people can do what they have always done. If it suits the resident, he or she can interact with house members or neighbors. Sometimes people will have a preference to have some private time watching TV because "It's what I do at my house."

UMC mindfully organized Avandell for the benefit of people with dementia. Outside of their houses, Avandell residents can move around freely within the safe, enclosed village square. They are welcome to visit shops, stop by the barn to see the goats and sheep, or chat with neighbors. The buildings and decorative architecture are meant to resemble a village, enough so people will feel comfortable being out and about. Avandell will always honor its residents' wishes of what they do and do not want, so there is very little difference in how people with us will live their daily lives. The rhythm of the day is close to the normal life they experienced throughout their lives.

We can provide many sorts of activities to engage people, but it will not be exactly in the same way UMC provides activities in its nursing home settings. People do not have to do the same activity at the same time or in the same place as everyone else. If exercise is needed, a staff member may encourage a resident to stand up out of their chair and move their muscles around.

Our nurse coordinator shared with me, "Maybe we'll redirect a resident out of the habit of too much isolation." Again, nothing is ever mandatory. Staff will be aware of which dementia residents prefer to spend time in their rooms and will "meet them where they are."

Susan Peterson told us that in their town, her mother Kathleen used to love to go shopping. She would run into friends and then they'd decide to get coffee. Freedom is what we provide for residents like Kathleen. Avandell recognizes the power of moments that fill our lives until we lose the mental and physical privilege to enjoy them. When you can't just pop out the door to do errands it can feel stifling. We all had been able to improvise during our days so why not continue feeling free and being normal. It makes such a difference for a person's happiness and independence, which notably reduces stress and gives people with dementia these special moments again.

In the village, residents will find a café, a grocery store, and a beauty salon. The businesses all resemble their real-life counterparts. Of course, they don't charge any money for goods or services. A resident can walk into the grocery store and buy a snack from the cashier, who is actually a trained memory care professional.

The main square has walkways where residents can move freely outside to green space. As I mentioned, Avandell's exterior yard is secure, so residents cannot leave the property's physical space. Otherwise, it's wide open like a park designed to have a variety of plants and flowers for intriguing experiences in the garden, such as in our butterfly section.

Avandell has medical facilities on the premises. We have a relationship with local hospitals, medical professionals, and municipal emergency services.

The essence of the environment is about creating a sense of home, peace, and community where everything people do is at their own pace.

BRAVE NEW WORLD

UMC is one of the first organizations to try the De Hogeweyk™ idea in the

US. We know now that there are villages being built in Canada, Australia, Italy, and the UK.

When we went to the Netherlands, we were invited to spend an entire day with the De Hogeweyk™ team. They were incredibly gracious and generous with their time and knowledge. We had so many questions, and they offered some truly fascinating insights into dementia care and what they had learned over the years. Of course, their perspective is a little different from ours because Holland has the benefit of socialized medicine, where taxes supplement the payment for care for its elders and all citizens.

For now, in the United States, Avandell will operate on a private pay basis. However, UMC is allocating 10% of the rooms for residents who have qualify for Medicaid. Consistent with UMC's benevolent mission, the Gift of Care Circle is available for residents who outlive their resources.

Our UMC group was inspired to learn how to manage a village. We were reminded of how Tapestries has enhanced the quality of UMC care as we grow our operations. We certainly encourage, respect and retain all of the little things that make life so much more normal and move away from traditional nursing home rules and settings.

Before we had Tapestries, we did not always have the luxury of focusing on niceties and social interaction that had always been part of a person's upbringing and daily life. In a more formal resident setting, institutions function without the sensitivity that Tapestries added to the enhancement of elder care. If you put Tapestries together with the philosophy of a village setting, there will be enormous success all around. Hence, Avandell.

De Hogeweyk™ truly inspired the UMC Tapestries team to establish its own dementia village. We began the process of building upon Tapestries with input from the Netherlands team. Founding Avandell made so much sense, and we committed that the village would be our next best step in providing care. Dementia care evolved, and we saw that the new model fit perfectly.

WE VALUE OUR RESIDENTS

It's tempting to look at the De Hogeweyk™ dementia village and think, "Build a new physical layout, add some gardens, and you're done." The truth is that while the physical aspects of Avandell are a major part of its design, the success of the model can only come from the core values that support the initiative.

We began the work of building Avandell. UMC was confident that our sense of stewardship and service were the best values to determine the success of the village concept. We added in the best of what we learned from De Hogeweyk™. Ultimately, both UMC and De Hogeweyk™ are on the same page, as both entities function with great compassion and respect for residents.

Avandell is not just a physical village. It's also a village in symbolic terms. It breaks down the institutional walls that have defined so much of dementia care for a number of generations.

UMC aligns the Tapestries model of memory care with Avandell's culture of freedom and normalcy. The new way of providing care gives a level of comfort to people and families. We are adopting new and different thinking about previous boundaries imposed on residents by rules and procedures. UMC is proud to have created its own village-like atmosphere. Residents have the freedom to live on their own terms and be themselves.

RELAXED CARE AND HAPPINESS ARE ENTIRELY POSSIBLE IN THE VILLAGE SETTING

Avandell views life as a tapestry—a weaving of all the threads from past events, past relationships, and past encounters. For the future of memory care in the United States, this revolutionary life model is the best we have ever seen. When residents and their families interact with Avandell they will discover an environment that infuses daily living with vitality and purpose.

Avandell invites residents to continue to weave their life's tapestry through things important to their identity. The goal is to have inspired days, even as some of life's moments are fleeting. The village is based on the idea of well-being, which, to Avandell, means that every aspect of life is considered, and through Avandell, UMC provides an authentic living experience that honors a resident's happiness.

Avandell features exceptionally designed housing built within the secure boundaries of a thriving community. Life's normal rhythms characterize the environment. Only at Avandell can a resident have a choice of leaving the house, walking to the grocery store, going to church, or eating at a restaurant. There is a community center where people can attend events and meetings along with outdoor parks and gardens to inspire, evoking peace, and serenity.

THE BENEFITS OF PLANNING

Going further, the benefits of Avandell help to inspire adult children who are caregivers and are very tired. Avandell helps families make the best choice for their parents. Families see new and better options for Mom or Dad to keep living the life they love without any major disruptions. At Avandell, building a new sort of senior living is based on UMC's commitment to providing residents the continuation of living their lives to the fullest.

The secret to making Avandell work is our respect for people and what makes them feel part of their own, chosen life. We acknowledge the concept of self and how that relates to our residents who have a dementia diagnosis. Even though the diagnosis is thought to rob a person of his or her own sense of self, part of a person's identity is still there—as various people living with dementia exist and manifest on different levels. We know that it is difficult for people with dementia to access short-term memory however, other parts of a person's life, especially their older memories, are easier to evoke. Music helps, and of course, feeling comfortable is crucial to creating a supportive and rich environment.

A sense of self is partly about an individual's personal identity, so continuity of that identity in a dementia care environment is helpful to preserve who someone is and always has been. It is important to create a living space that reflects people's individuality.

Some of the comforting ways we can reassure people with dementia and not disrupt their "life's familiarity" is to design relatable interiors and build in personal touches that remind people of their lifelong style of living. The mindful structural design of a residence, familiar furniture of a certain era, and other stylistic touches enhance the living experience. Attention to what people need is how Avandell makes moving to the village seamless. We are dedicated to helping residents feel at home because the village resembles all things familiar with homes that seem like their own.

A sense of self is also about community and preferred social interaction, hobbies, interests, and even a lifetime of professional or family experience. If you lived in a town where you always saw your friends at the bakery or café, you would not feel quite like yourself if the only place you could socialize is the memory care floor of a hospital-like building. Avandell is different. It seeks to restore these missing elements that people need.

A SENSE OF HOME

Our industry had long embraced old and outdated ideas of how residents should live, but we found that offering seniors "nursing homes" and "rest homes" was not enough of the real thing and a scenario that could disrupt function for people with dementia. They don't deal very well with change. The traditional facilities would not resemble the homes they knew for countless years, but a village like Avandell with homes and stores helps them have a more comfortable transition.

The village setting has pretty houses with colorful interiors that feel like home. Thomas would appreciate the atmosphere because home in Avandell is normal to Thomas. The houses feature different styles of décor. Some are modern, rustic, or traditional. Others will have antiques that may resemble pieces that might have been in the person's actual home and increase their comfort level as they live among familiar things.

If Judith were to arrange for Thomas to become a resident at Avandell, he would enter a new home set up to resemble the type of home he already lived in. Judith told us their home was old-fashioned and decorated with colonial-style furniture. We can do that. Avandell will have a house that is old-fashioned with a familiar, neighborhood style. Avandell residents who lived in more modern homes will find a house provides contemporary finishes like stone, glass, metal, and polished nickel.

The architects of Avandell understand and respect our inspiration from the village in the Netherlands and how we combine that with the culture of weaving in Tapestries.

Designers anticipated the needs of people with dementia and gave UMC a balanced, friendly, productive and curated environment. They crafted residences and public buildings that feel much more like home than a memory care floor for twenty-five people—with bland, identical rooms.

The best atmosphere minimizes stress for a resident like Thomas. We help him keep his usual routine while he lives in a physical setting that reminds him of the house where he lived before. He will be cohabitating with people he probably would have been friends with. It's all about experiencing his familiar or his normal.

For Thomas and all of our residents, we will do our best to arrange housemates with similar interests or backgrounds. Thomas was always in the company of professors and scientists, so we knew he would feel more at home with educated people who reminded him of his intellectual background.

THE BEAUTY AND PURPOSE OF SURROUNDING OURSELVES IN NATURE

In our experience, nature is a powerful force for helping people with dementia find tranquility and familiarity. The lack of nature is one of the great deficiencies in most institutional memory care facilities. This is mostly a problem of structural design. A traditional institution keeps people from really enjoying the outdoors.

Decoration does not provide enough nature, and residents deserve to be outside. Indoor potted plants are not enough. Ceilings painted blue with clouds don't work. Neither do faux circa 1950s streetscapes. People with a dementia diagnosis need to experience the weather: sun, rain, and snow. Avandell is including this natural environment to create a new level of familiarity. At Avandell, they are safe and protected as they stroll around their village and meet their neighbors.

The gardens are planned to provide several distinct, natural settings. We hired a leading landscape architect to design a bird and butterfly garden for our first Avandell project. There will be fun, interactive outdoor spaces featuring a sculpture garden, interesting wind and sound experiences, and a rock and water garden. Another feature we offer is a greenhouse where residents can grow and pick herbs for their lunch or dinner or visit a unique sensory garden.

Avandell's nature offerings will be a special addition to the memory care experience. UMC knows the importance of greenspace, and we always include beautiful, natural settings in our other communities. For example, our Bristol Glen community in Newton, New Jersey, sits on seventy-four wooded acres. Residents there can join in gardening activities or just enjoy the grounds.

THE ACTIVITY PAVILION

Avandell features a pavilion and other lovely public spaces dedicated to activities and special experiences. The activity pavilion will have a community room for events, games, and club activities that add to the harmony of the day. The plan is to have dedicated club rooms. The idea is to visit the community space and not feel that it is too reminiscent of a traditional nursing home setting.

There will be areas where people can enjoy music, art, exercise, musical performances and other things they loved before a dementia diagnosis. Avandell will celebrate what's meaningful and normal for each individual. For example, because it is important to many people, we will invite children's choirs, amateur performers, and some professional shows. The art club will have art shows featuring resident's pottery, painting, and collage.

SPIRITUALITY

UMC is an organization founded on Christian principles. We integrate a meaningful sense of spirituality into how we approach our work, stressing compassion, kindness, and respect with residents, families, and staff. It is important for older adults to have the opportunity to engage in religious worship or comparable spiritual practices.

For this reason, we envision the spiritual space as an environment for worship services. The space will feel familiar for multiple traditions, including Judaism, Islam, and various Christian denominations. The expression of daily spiritual traditions will be honored and encouraged. Avandell's chaplain will provide pastoral care and counseling, and build relationships with religious leaders of all faiths.

MENTAL HEALTH

Mental health needs for dementia residents and their families are important and Avandell's staff will be prepared. In the process of joining UMC, staff are aware of emotional needs—it is woven into the process of researching the resident and the family during the transition into the village setting.

We find that the change is harder on the family. Residents are so much more resilient than their family believes. Avandell will be connected to support groups, and we will suggest referrals to other agencies and information whenever the opportunity arises. We will connect to the Alzheimer's Association, workshops, family council, and care plan meetings.

The community building has a space dedicated to educational resources and informative programs. The room will serve as a venue for meetings with residents, as well as with members of the outside community. It might be used for an Alzheimer's Association family support group. We plan to engage with healthcare providers in the area and industry peers. Avandell wants to share what we've learned, and all are welcome.

COMMUNITY RESOURCES

In the spirit of sharing what works, I've learned that it is a great idea to see how other industries and professional disciplines solved their biggest challenges. There is so much wisdom and experience in the world, which is exactly what Tapestries is helping us incorporate into a fulfilling daily life for our residents. For example, I am motivated by how Volvo decided years ago to share its seat belt technology. They provided the first seat belt and then shared the design with other car companies for free.

Volvo's goal was to improve auto safety. They could have made money licensing the patent for the seat belt, but they accomplished more important objectives by sharing the design. Their move saved hundreds of thousands of lives around the world. You can't put a dollar value on that. By popularizing seat belts, Volvo has built one of the world's most respected brands, and when people think of a safe car, most people will say Volvo. The business lesson is that giving away seat belts for free garnered Volvo respect and has been worth billions to the company.

The inspiration for Avandell fits with what Volvo did. We believe that we can help other providers of dementia care build similar programs. UMC is committed to sharing our knowledge to benefit the overall industry, and we think that at the same time it will help our brand. It's a win-win.

STAFFING

It takes the right people to care for those with dementia. Avandell has an approach to staffing that grew from developing Tapestries. UMC will take the best from what we've learned and apply achievements to enhance Avandell. However, there will be some notable differences.

The buildings and layout are different. Staff will learn to adapt through specialized training in the environment. An example of the change is that each family house will have two dedicated staff members during the day. This is similar to what we have with Tapestries but more intense and focused. It will be a bit like living in a home with relatives. In addition to the basics of dementia care, staff members will be in charge of organizing meals and coordinating activities.

One of these daytime staff will be a household coordinator who will be in the house each day they work. Essential responsibilities include meal planning and preparation, shopping, and overseeing household responsibilities like medication administration. The houses will also have a Certified Nurse Assistant, or CNA, during the day and evening with shared CNA staff overnight. These staff members will be cross-trained for dining, to make and serve all meals and housekeeping.

The household-centric nature of Avandell creates a need for staff coordination. We will have daily household meetings and weekly neighborhood meetings to review resident and household needs.

This may seem like a lot, but in reality, what I've covered here are just a few of the core elements of the Avandell model. In the next chapter, I'll discuss how we are putting the concept into action.

CHAPTER 9

REALIZING THE AVANDELL VISION

When you manage a large organization, as I do, you have to come to terms with the reality that at some point, after all the talk, all the envisioning and all the thinking, if you want to turn an idea into a reality, you have to take action. This may sound obvious, but I've been doing this long enough to understand two often difficult facts about this process. First, sometimes you never actually take action steps. The idea remains an idea, untested and perfect as an unrealized concept. Second, when you do take action, things may not go as you imagined.

To avoid the second difficulty, it is necessary to plan for the operationalization of your idea. Things may not turn out as you hoped, but the planning process will have done its job and set up the beginnings. Planning is essential and sets the stage for the inevitable changes and challenges that come your way.

To take all the ideas we had for Avandell and turn them into an operational reality was a huge challenge. In this endeavor, I had the privilege of tapping into the wisdom and support of a team of trusted experts. This chapter discusses the steps we are taking to operationalize the Avandell concept.

The only way to demonstrate the efficacy of the Avandell model is to show a real, functioning example of the idea. We decided to take this step for Avandell.

The plan for Avandell is, located on an 18.5-acre site, where 105 residents will live in 15 houses of 7 residents each. The houses will be set in distinct neighborhoods, each with its own varied, lush landscape. In addition to the houses, there will be a Town Center, Activity Pavilion, and barn. The amenity spaces will be open to the residents, family, friends and organized groups, with people of all ages encouraged to visit and interact.

Digital rendering of the pilot site for the Avandell concept, showing the Town Square on the left and the Activity Pavilion (the red structure).

Avandell promises both indoor and outdoor experiences for residents. The Town Center and village green are planned to be the heart of Avandell, where residents leave the privacy of their houses to gather together as a broader community. Weather permitting, we expect residents will enjoy spending time on the green, in the adjacent sensory gardens, and visiting, and maybe even caring for, the animals in the barn. The houses that surround the village green are about the same distance from the Town Square and Activity Pavilion.

Architect's rendering of the bistro and main Town Square building.

The "Village Green" at Avandell, showing the Activity Pavilion on the right.

Rendering of an Avandell site, showing the natural environment and outdoor paths.

THE ARCHITECTURAL PERSPECTIVE: DESIGN AND OPERATIONS

Taking a concept like Avandell and rendering it in three dimensions in the real world was a challenge that required the services of some very talented and experienced architects. In this, I did not have to take much time to think about whom I wanted to hire. In fact, they were already on speed dial.

UMC has been incredibly fortunate over the years to have as its architectural partner the respected design firm of Perkins Eastman, PE for short. The firm believes that design should have a positive impact on the quality of people's lives and their surrounding environment. We continue to develop and expand on our great working relationship with two of its senior living designers and architects, David Hoglund and Max Winters, who, from their expert architectural perspective, have spent much of their professional lives searching out the best ways for an aging population to live and thrive. This pair, backed by the resources of the firm, is directly responsible for the success and newly designed vision that has made Avandell possible.

I feel David and Max's perspectives on how we took Avandell off the white board and turned it into a shovel-ready project were worth an extended deep dive. To that end, I actually interviewed them. The following includes excerpts from that interview.

The seeds of UMC's dementia village concepts and inspirations for Avandell developed from David and Max's professional and personal dedication, experience, and ability to think outside of the box. It took great creativity, imagination, and open minds to see new possibilities for living and working in our new village concept.

My professional relationship with David and Perkins Eastman dates back decades. I worked with them on other architectural projects over the span of my career in senior living. One of the reasons I like working with David so much is his explanation of the architect's role.

As he put it, "You think architects are hired to design buildings. We are not. We are hired to solve problems." That's the essence of how UMC's partnership with Perkins Eastman evolved over the years.

"We have problems we need to solve. Through dialogue and the design process, we arrive at solutions in the form of innovative structures and design features to make life better and easier."

BRAINSTORMING OUR WAY OUT OF THE INSTITUTIONAL APPROACH TO DESIGN

Max and David worked closely with UMC to imagine what would raise the quality of care and make a difference in the lives of people with dementia. They codified and created Avandell from inspiration and research around what the best life for those living with dementia could and should be.

We held a number of workshops. The goal was to arrive at a fresh concept for how to live with dementia in a different type of space. UMC and the PE teams brainstormed around the next iteration of dementia residences and what that would mean in the architectural sense—what PE calls the "built environment." We took ideas from Tapestries and De Hogeweyk™, powered by PE's years of experience, to fit together the best ideas to launch a new paradigm.

The Perkins Eastman team went to Holland. Next, it was the UMC team's turn to go. Max explained, "David and I, and some of our colleagues, had traveled to De Hogeweyk™. Coincidentally, another colleague of mine was speaking about the dementia village idea and posted about it on LinkedIn. You saw her post and said to David and me, 'This story about the dementia village is really interesting and exciting. Can you talk to us about this?' That was the beginning of the beginning where the bigger idea began to emerge."

Like so many people who are involved in caring for older people, Max first became interested in the subject through his own family experience. He said, "I had always been interested in senior living and more so while I was working on my architecture degree. At the same time, I was seeing what my grandparents were going through and how the possibilities of various built environments related to the needs of the evolution of aging. I received my Master of Architecture at the University of Cincinnati and did my thesis on senior living. I gravitated to the architectural firm of Perkins Eastman because of their reputation and quality of their work."

David also gave his take on the journey, sharing, "I started much the same way Max did. I was interested in the topic of senior living in graduate school, probably more generally, as I examined the impact on special populations and housing settings. I first worked on low-income housing projects and some housing for substance abuse, as well as environments for emotionally, physically, and intellectually challenged kids. But senior living became my passion, and I was fortunate in 1981 to land a post-graduate fellowship to go to Europe for four months and study what was happening in the senior space, particularly in the northern European countries. I came back, wrote a book about it, and have spent my entire career involved in senior living."

The workshops were focused on the "What's next," but we realized we were still somewhat mired in the "What's now." David said, "As architects and developers, we had to be wary of the redundancy of being caught in the sorts of the things we already knew, meaning that designs were too close to what was already out there. The question and challenge was, 'How do we think differently about it?'"

David worked previously on Woodside Place, one of the first dementia-specific environments in the United States. The facility and its innovative mission were recognized in the media and in the senior care industry. His new ideas inspired colleagues to think about how people with cognitive challenges could live together in comfort and dignity.

According to David, "I think we've replicated that model a lot. What led to the development of Avandell with Tapestries woven in was, 'Where do we go next?' We all had to rethink things we already knew and had already done. In an institutional model like this, there needs to be very clear answers to those questions. There are a lot of working parts, and those are almost always answered around convenience, replication, and efficiency."

The early part of the design process was extremely collaborative between UMC and the PE team. Max characterized our dialogue stating, "In some pieces of the weaving of the concepts we were not creating ideas out of whole cloth—but almost whole cloth. We did a lot of process mapping with you and his team, and we would keep going back to the drawing board to discuss something as simple as, 'Where does the trash go, how does it leave the house, who picks it up?' The process mindfully had us all collaborating and walking through details step-by-step."

Max and David describe their general approach to design as "humanist." Perkins Eastman refers to this as "human by design," a phrase that captures the goal of serving people to help them live out their best lives in new living situations. This design ethos is critical to success in PE's senior living practice. Max said, "It's something that we take pretty darn seriously, which in architecture is a tool to make the lives of people better. It's not just an art form for its own sake."

He contrasted the design process used for Avandell with the institutional approach to hospital design used in the past. Max said, "I think that one of the difficulties with past hospital design, which continues to inform lots of present nursing home design, is that hospital buildings can represent

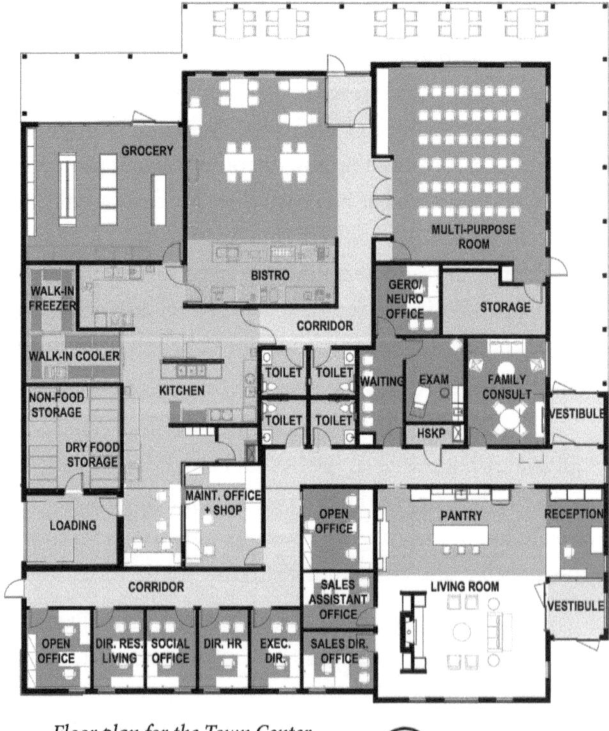

Floor plan for the Town Center

the authority of the institution. If you go into a hospital, there are many restrictions and rules. A lot of the time, the rules are literally designed into the structure, as in, 'You can't go here or go there.' The new dementia village is almost the opposite in philosophy because people are allowed to go and walk around. As you say, 'Avandell says yes more than it says no.' In this case, you are opening up the space for people and de-emphasizing institutional authority in the structure."

Max continued, "What we've been trying to change is to eliminate the idea of institution and the regimentation. Whether the reference is school or the military, you get up at a set time, meals are always at the same time, etc. That is what we're trying to depart from—to allow people to live the way they always have in their personal, individual life cycles."

This thinking informs the design of the courtyard, which celebrates winds and breezes. Residents will see birdhouses and things that move in the wind. We also have decorative grasses that move. The pleasant types of different things that move are complimented by auditory cues that help to orient so residents know where they are. It is subtle but part of the bigger plan to celebrate residents' time outdoors.

Some of the dialogue about reminiscence in the design of existing memory care environments is a bit too focused on the visual and the image aspects. This goes back to what we were saying earlier about nostalgia. Research has shown that reminiscence is often more about physical actions and other sensory experiences. Sound, smell, and touch are significant aspects that can trigger a memory or engage someone in reminiscence beyond just the image or the visual.

Floor plan for the Activity Pavilion

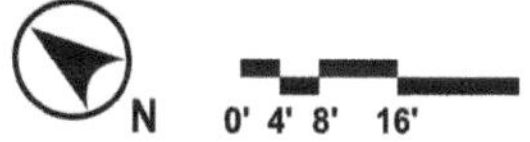

Color also plays a role in the experience of Avandell. The Activity Pavilion in the middle of the main courtyard can be seen from each of the house courtyards. It will be painted farm red, so it becomes a landmark as residents move throughout the everyday elements and locations in the village. This is very much the same concept of how older, traditional towns and villages have a steeple on the church in the center of town or cupola on the town hall.

The houses will be in different colors, but what really matters are things like porches and mailboxes to create individual properties. There may be different materials on the trim, rocking chairs, or decorative stones. So, we're not simply having a blue house and a gray one. Some houses may be decorated with reclaimed wood or brick.

Here is where we can make the homes unique and different, without cookie-cutter colors. Maybe the mailboxes are on the house or on a post in the front of the house. All the mailboxes can be different, so that this becomes, again, one of those devices that normalize where people with dementia will live.

SCALE AND RELATIONSHIPS BETWEEN BUILT SPACES

When you work with an architect, their first deliverable is usually a sketch, followed by a more detailed rendering of what the exterior of a building is going to look like, along with its internal spaces. However, having worked with PE before, I understood that these drawings represented the end of a very deep thought process. There's so much you don't see.

In our case, the workshops moved on to the subject of how the single houses would function internally. We also discussed how houses could come together to form neighborhoods that could easily relate to one another. This required, according to Max, thinking "about different scales and the relationships between buildings." The PE team calls them "precedents." The architects looked at actual drawings for design inspiration.

There were three key ideas that Max and David highlighted that were really important to UMC's vision:

"The first was the Methodist Camp meeting towns. This is a ubiquitous precedent that planners and architects involved in communities will look

Methodist Camp meeting, ca – 1850

at. It's of particular interest to us at UMC, as it's part of our heritage. It was really inspiring to understand that the Methodist faith has long focused on bringing people together in physical communities. Now, we are taking this idea into our era to help people with dementia. The value here is looking at how people organically form a community and then how they relate to each other. We wanted to build on that archetype idea in Avandell.

Second, we were also looking at Shaker villages, thinking about how the buildings relate to the landscape. The third precedent or archetype is from the Netherlands and is similar. It's called the Hofjes—courtyard-facing buildings that were meant to support marginalized populations. An example would be a comfortable and convenient atmosphere for widows or widowers. These little enclaves all face into a common courtyard."

As David elaborated, "We took a historical look and overview about how people in a residential or in a camp meeting version of community—more temporary residential settings—naturally configure their spaces or form groups. These courtyards were really helpful and influenced the final design."

Architect's sketch that explores relationships between built space and the natural environment.

This may seem rather esoteric, but it is exactly this sort of thinking that leads to design breakthroughs like we're getting with Avandell. It's a multidimensional thought process. How does the household relate to its residents? How does the neighborhood relate to itself? How does the entire village relate to itself? And how do you function within each of those things? The sketch shown here depicts how the architects work through this thought process.

Dutch Hofjes courtyard in Haarlem - Picture taken by Guus Bosman on September 14th, 2004.

The process also incorporates what architects and designers call "biophilic design," which is design with natural elements to boost occupant health and well-being. Biophilic design is about the relationship between the built environment and the natural environment. How does the design mimic nature? There was a lot of discussion about the relationship between the landscape spaces and the buildings, how to form neighborhoods, and how to give them varied identities. Each of the courtyards will take on a different personality.

According to David, "We were inspired to bring in the four elements. Spaces are a little bit more interpretive to give each of these landscape spaces a different feel while staying away from being too literal. As architects and designers, part of our psyches can be trapped in what we've previously known and built, so initially, our training led to conceptualizing Avandell as a building that had rooms organized along traditional staffing patterns. That meant there would be fourteen to sixteen people living in a wing or a house, or perhaps a cluster or neighborhood—again, traditional words. Max and I really took those concepts about as far as we could and realized nothing was really new and certainly not unique enough."

David and Max began to talk about what they could learn from what other architects, builders, and companies were doing. This inspired the two of them to, as they put it, "begin creating a life experience for people with cognitive challenges that could still be interesting and provocative in a positive way."

Team members from PE and UMC, along with consultants involved in developing concepts that would lead to Avandell, began getting excited about the energy of the project, creating not only a place to provide really comfortable housing and support for people with cognitive challenges and dementia, but also the larger village environment.

NORMALIZING LIFE

For Max, the biggest takeaway from seeing the dementia village model was thinking about what happens for somebody with a dementia diagnosis when they walk outside of their primary buildings. Having worked on other projects that represented a refinement and replication of the Woodside Village model, he now focused on expanding the concept, thinking about the small house and how that sort of building could be more normal and feel truly residential compared with traditional institutional dementia housing.

Thinking about the dementia village put David firmly in his problem-solver role. He saw a challenge facing UMC in terms of messaging. He said, "The whole senior living industry is presumed to be about sending your loved ones to a place where you're expecting certain institutional approaches to safety, security, and care. The customer, that adult child, often has not given thought to the risks of their loved one staying at home and how those risks compare to going into a congregate living environment."

We have entirely reframed that question to now be, "How do we have a place where people with dementia can live the normal life they have always known?" Obviously, people are going to be safe in Avandell, but from the beginning of planning, we prioritized the complete experience.

Seeing De Hogeweyk™ was critical to the evolution of Max's and David's thinking about the resident experience. In particular, they resonated with the positive experience of its residents and observed what happens when people are between buildings or outside of a building. The architects had long been focused on skilled nursing settings and the buildings themselves.

> De Hogeweyk™ gave David and Max a view of the potential upside and scale of, in their words, "How does the village setting create a more holistic experience for someone with dementia? There's actually a public realm available to them, where they can go and experience life beyond just the four walls of their house. That was our big 'aha' moment. After having seen De Hogeweyk™, that was the beginning of how we designed Avandell."

For Max, the word "village" evokes the experience we're trying to create. A village has places where you live, places where you worship, places where you shop, and places where you do other things. In an overnight workshop, which resulted in Avandell, participants tried to label what we were developing. Someone on the team suggested, "Well, it's sort of like an enclave," so Enclave (any small, distinct area or group enclosed or isolated within a large one) became the working title for the village concept. We've since renamed the village Avandell. The point is, we wanted something that had a positive sense of comfort, safety, and insularity.

Avandell uses built space, nature and the spaces between buildings to begin to replicate patterns of normal life. Max spoke to this point about normalizing life, saying, "Some of our process had to do with the fact that, as a village, Avandell wasn't going to be in one traditional, expected building. Because some of the experience would truly be outside, people kept saying, 'Well, you need to put a roof over the whole thing, or if you are trying to achieve a sense of the sky, maybe paint the ceiling blue and put clouds on it.'" However, part of the normalized village life is to experience the weather. When it snows in New Jersey, people are going to experience the snow. This might complicate our life a little bit because they're going to put a coat on, and they're going to have to watch out for ice. Of course, I'm going to insist on heated sidewalks so we don't have people slipping on ice, but a true village means inside and outside living.

Thinking through "normal" was an important part of the design process. And, as we discovered, normal is not just about built space. It's about things like food. The incorporation of the grocery store element and the idea that houses will essentially shop for the ingredients that they use to cook is really important for a kind of normal food rhythm.

What does that mean for the grocery store and for the households? How does everything get transported? All of these different considerations impact how Avandell operates, so the design has to accommodate day-to-day functioning across the board.

One workshop we did was called "What's the house like?" It led us to a bedroom design, and we came up with the idea of a bay window where one might have a puzzle table. Residents could have a piano or an art easel, too. How would we take this idea of the individual experience and apply it to a shared space with six other people? When you step outside of your house, you're sharing the outside spaces with your neighbors. Then we looked at things in all those different scales and how some of them overlap.

We know it's going to be different in each house, and some people aren't going to want to go shopping. The challenge is to design Avandell to provide an abundant life for all levels of cognitive ability. We want to make it both an experience and a challenge each day to get outside and experience something approximating normal life.

ENVISIONING RESIDENTS' LIVES

Life is more normal at Avandell, and schedules are truly up to the residents. A daily schedule of breakfast at 7, lunch at 12, and so forth is not what Avandell will subscribe to. The lives of residents will be largely up to them. Of course, certain daily operations processes are pre-programmed. The dentist visits on certain days. The cleaning crews are active at specific hours. Otherwise, the daily life of a resident is relatively free-flowing.

For one thing, the house structure at Avandell is fluid and impacts the schedule and daily life of each resident, subject to the needs of a small group of people. Instead of arranging for twenty-one or more residents on a "unit" or floor, the house only has to handle the needs of seven people. As we envision it, residents will be able to go to bed and get up when they want. Meal service will be flexible. The dedicated staff members in the house will make sure that each resident gets up, gets dressed, and eats. If someone wants to sleep late, they can.

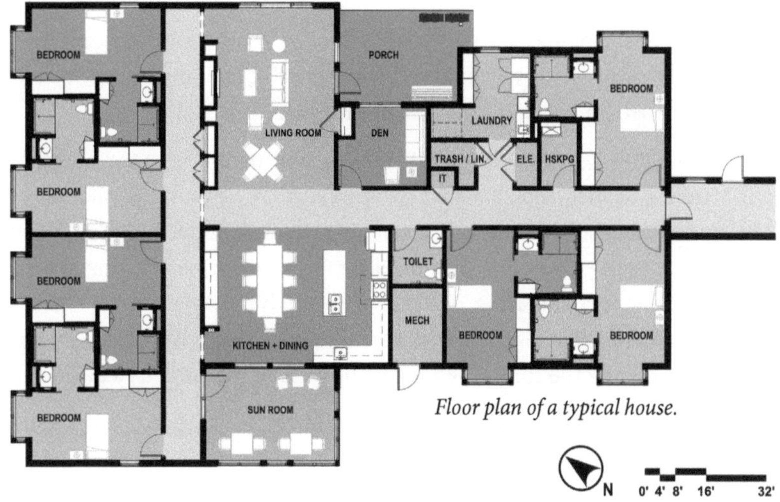

Floor plan of a typical house.

A resident's life at Avandell centers around the house and his or her individual room. The design philosophy for residents' rooms, as advanced by the PE team, is "room to be yourself." Though powered by smart home technology, the houses are crafted to feel natural for a non-technical resident. Each room has a sitting area, a window with an alcove, a closet, and a private bathroom. The window alcove might contain a bookcase or a writing desk—touches that invite the resident to engage in activities that will feel familiar, even if the resident is not entirely capable of enjoying them as he or she did in the past. What matters is the opportunity to engage in normal life and stimulate sensory memories.

The house, shown in the floorplan, mixes public and private spaces. The public spaces include a living room, kitchen/dining room, and den. In keeping with the drive for familiarity and normality, the architects suggested open shelving displays in the dining area, shown in the sketch. The idea is to mimic the appearance of a real house, where people may show their dishes and little items that suggest home. The dishes and other items on display will also reinforce the lifestyle of the house: modern for modern, traditional for traditional, and so forth. The den is envisioned as a

Floor plan of a typical house.

semi-private area in the public space, perhaps for private conversations or quiet time outside the resident's actual room. A front porch opens onto an exterior courtyard. A screened-in porch is available in the back of the house.

After breakfast, a resident might want to venture out into the Town Square. This might be just to take a walk around and say hello to people. They can get a coffee at the bistro, get their hair cut, or pick up food for lunch at the supermarket. Or they can engage in a club meeting. This might mean doing a fitness routine, participating in an art class, or music club. Club meetings have a schedule, but we expect that a resident who is interested in doing an activity will be able to find one available during the time when he or she goes to the Activity Pavilion.

Residents will find music, if that's what they're looking for at a given moment. It may be an organized music program, a musical visitor engaging with a resident, or an impromptu singalong at the piano. This is what we saw at De Hogeweyk™, so we've designed the opportunity for music into Avandell.

Residents will have the ability to explore outside, and we hope they do. In a conventional dementia care setting, a resident wandering off and getting lost is a huge problem. Here, it's an opportunity. We've designed the site to make it nearly impossible for a resident to get outside the secure perimeter. Inside the perimeter but outdoors, residents will find themselves with a variety of natural environments to experience. They can see birds and butterflies, hear wind and sound, listen to the water flowing over rocks, or take in sculptures.

Lunch and dinner are back at the house, followed by whatever activities residents want to do. Bedtime is when residents choose it to be. If residents have medical appointments or a specific requirement, such as physical therapy, on any given day staff will guide them to it. Otherwise, resident life at Avandell will be pretty much what residents make of it.

THE FAMILY AND COMMUNITY EXPERIENCE AT AVANDELL

Avandell is designed to accommodate visitors. We expect family members to visit loved ones, of course, but we also anticipate engagement with members of the local community and our professional peers in the elder care field. Most of the public spaces at Avandell have been designed to meet the needs of residents and visitors alike.

The Town Center and Activity Pavilion, in particular, are set up so visitors can experience the community together. A child might visit a parent and go to eat at the bistro, for example. They might sit outside together and take in the natural environment. Seating areas will be sized and spaced for this use. The house dens accommodate personal meetings between residents and visitors.

The barn and greenhouse are places that will help residents and visitors enjoy one another's company. For example, we think these spaces will allow for an experience that's much needed but difficult to achieve in a traditional environment, which is the connection between residents, their grandchildren, and great grandchildren. We have seen this so often: adult children bring grandchildren, or great grandchildren to visit. The children quickly get bored or turned off by the presence of very elderly, detached people with whom they can't speak. The visits don't last long, and no one is particularly happy. Now, we can change this dynamic for the better.

At Avandell, we have the space and facilities to let visiting children enjoy themselves (under supervision, of course) while grandparent residents can enjoy seeing the children. They don't have the ability to ask, "How's school?" or "What's your favorite sport?" anymore, but they can still get the pleasure and life-affirming experience of the normality we strive for by seeing their extended families in natural life settings. We suspect we will be seeing more than a few children's birthday parties taking place in the barn.

THE AVANDELL TECH CENTER

We envision Avandell as a destination for elder care professionals who want to learn more about how the Avandell model works. To this end, we imagine the multi-purpose room at the Town Center and Tech Center, shown in the image, will serve as the location for presentations and professional development programs.

Avandell staff will give tours, much in the same way the leaders of De Hogeweyk™ gave of their time to help us understand what they were accomplishing when we visited.

UMC is in discussions with a wide variety of nearby medical professionals and institutions regarding partnerships that will benefit them and our residents. They are already aware of our long history of successfully serving the aging population in New Jersey, and Avandell is set up to facilitate new partnerships with the professional community. We can transport residents to their sites or have visiting professionals work with residents in our own exam rooms and family consult rooms.

Avandell is available for community events, as well, including ones that are not specific to our program. If a local organization wants to use our multi-purpose room for a meeting, we are excited about the opportunity to make it available.

Community engagement is also one of our priorities. We may host school field trips or scout troops. We are reaching out to local schools to see if there is interest in volunteering. We are already having great success with these sorts of ideas in our other communities. Local churches have reached out to us expressing an interest in creating a ministry dedicated to caring for elder residents. We are thrilled at this prospect. It's exactly the kind of relationship we think will benefit everyone involved—the church, our program, the residents, and their families.

As you can see, a project like Avandell doesn't just happen. It's the result of an enormous amount of thinking, planning, and doing. The smallest detail might be the result of extensive brainstorming and analytical processes. From "Where does the garbage go?" and "How does the food get into the house?" to "How can we emulate a Methodist camp meeting?"

We have arrived at this profoundly different physical space for helping people with dementia form a community. The plans are finished. Everyone is excited to make a difference in a new, more natural community of care. We are now in the process of getting the project approved for construction. Hopefully, by the time you're reading this book, we'll be available to show you around in person.

CONCLUSION

At the beginning of this book, we met the Millers and the Petersons, who were families experiencing the common challenges that arise from a dementia diagnosis. Many adult children and partners minimize and dismiss moments of confusion or strange behavior as a series of benign senior moments. Short-term memory loss, frustration, and forgetting how to care of oneself are signs that a person might need expert help, specifically professional care in a safe environment.

Because families are experiencing lives in transition, they visit UMC communities and comparable providers to look for options for care. We offer a quality of life that suits the needs of people who have trouble with thinking. If the Millers and Petersons had come to us twenty years ago, their choices would have been quite different from what's available now.

Over the years, the elder care industry has evolved to be more person-centric, moving away from the use of physical and chemical restraints. Today, a family can choose between assisted living and a range of more structured and intensive care options. It's possible, or even advisable, for a family to plan for in-home memory care and the eventual move into a memory care residence as their loved one's needs increase over time.

As we shared, a few years back we began to ask some fundamental, probing questions about how we approached a resident's experience. Open to challenging, any and all, assumptions, we pushed ourselves to think of ways to enable residents to live their fullest possible lives, despite the diagnosis of dementia. What has proven to be a stubborn problem in dementia care is the ability to give residents a normal and authentic life. We have learned that minimizing a person's stress and distress mitigates the negative behaviors that can otherwise manifest. How could we better honor the humanity of a person? This process resulted in our Tapestries program.

When we visited De Hogeweyk™, we found ourselves inspired to weave our Tapestries approach into a new, American paradigm. UMC gathered experts who came together and identified the needs of aging dementia populations. The team was tasked to design and build a familiar and safe space that resembled the village we now know to be Avandell.

Many residents and adult children have told us that, throughout their lives, they feared losing their independence or dignity in situations that did not respect who they were before the onset of dementia. In Avandell, people will be free to experience life on their own terms. We are weaving in the best parts of life and celebrating a new set of colors and textures with our residents.

Avandell creates an opportunity for residents to live in a community designed just for them. We will let people continue to be themselves with minimal guidance from staff. The idea of a pleasant functioning village that is similar to a resident's previous living situation is quite different from the older institutional paradigm.

Avandell will take advantage of all the latest research in serving memory care residents. While there is still no way to reverse the course of the disease, science has provided many insights into the best ways to help individuals, families, and caregivers live their best possible lives.

While Avandell will be part of UMC's portfolio of senior living communities, our vision is actually far broader and more ambitious. We are doing this to help the entire senior living industry take a step forward in how they work with people with dementia.

Avandell has been conceived as a showcase for today's most outstanding ideas in dementia care. We are actively planning to share our designs and plans with other providers across the U.S. Early feedback from peer organizations has been overwhelmingly positive.

The public will also benefit from Avandell. We will have a community center with resources to meet the growing need for dementia care. The Neurocognitive Clinic and Resource Hub will form a Center of Excellence for assessment, training, and education. It will offer strategies and tools to help families caring for a loved one at home.

Avandell is leading the way in reinventing the dementia experience. We are proud to support this vulnerable, growing population, and hope to inspire the senior living industry to provide an authentic and normal experience for residents, families, caregivers, and dear friends.

ABOUT THE AUTHOR

Larry Carlson was the President & CEO of United Methodist Communities (UMC) for eleven years before his retirement. Larry's career in senior living spans more than forty-five years, having served in leadership roles for six not-for-profit, faith-driven organizations in four states.

Larry has diverse and extensive experience in multiple aspects of eldercare administration. His expertise includes CCRC, long-term skilled nursing, post-acute rehabilitation, congregate housing, adult day health, memory care, and assisted living. He is skilled in operations, strategic planning, board development, new project design and development, construction, and start-ups. During Larry's career, he championed and implemented many diverse and innovative business strategies and programs to better the lives of those he served.

As a newlywed at twenty-three, Larry and his wife Melanie lived five years in a not-for-profit, community-based nursing facility in Boston as he began his career. Today, Melanie and Larry, married forty-eight years, are "crazy" for their three daughters and four grandchildren.

Published by

TVGUESTPERT PUBLISHING

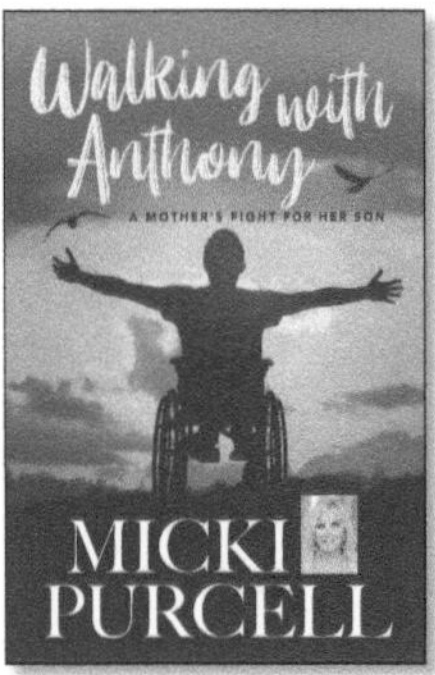

MICKI PURCELL
Walking With Anthony: A Mother's Fight For Her Son
Hardcover $22.95
Kindle: $9.99

SHEILA H. FORMAN, Ph.D
Tame Your Appetite: The Art of Mindful Eating
Paperback: $16.95
Kindle: $9.99

SHEILA H. FORMAN, Ph.D
Mindful Bite, Joyful Life: 365 Days of Mindful Eating
Paperback: $22.95
Kindle: $9.99

IAN WINER
Ubiquitous Relativity: My Truth is Not the Truth
Paperback: $16.95
Kindle: $9.99

DARREN CAMPO
Alex Detail's Revolution
Paperback: $9.95
Hardcover: $22.95
Kindle: $9.15

DARREN CAMPO
Alex Detail's Rebellion
Hardcover: $22.95
Kindle: $9.99

DARREN CAMPO
Disappearing Spell: Generationist Files: Book 1
Kindle: $2.99

DARREN CAMPO
Stingers
Paperback: $9.99
Kindle: $9.99

TVGuestpert Publishing
11664 National Blvd, #345
Los Angeles, CA. 90064
310-584-1504
www.TVGPublishing.com

JOANNA DODD MASSEY
Culture Shock: Surviving Five Generations in One Workplace
Paperback: $16.95
Kindle/Nook: $9.99

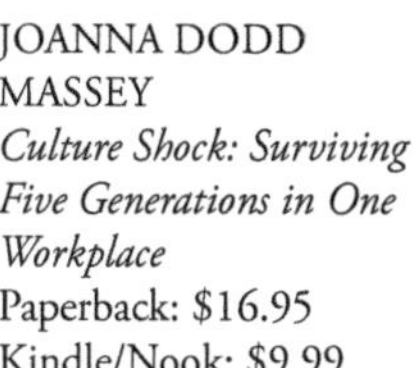

JACQUIE JORDAN AND SHANNON O'DOWD
*The Ultimate On-Camera Guidebook: Hosts*Experts*Influencers*
Paperback: $16.95
Kindle: $9.99

JACQUIE JORDAN
Heartfelt Marketing: Allowing the Universe to Be Your Business Partner
Paperback: $15.95
Kindle: $9.99
Audible: $9.95

JACQUIE JORDAN
Get on TV! The Insider's Guide to Pitching the Producers and Promoting Yourself
Published by Sourcebooks
Paperback: $14.95
Kindle: $9.99
Nook: $14.95

GAYANI DESILVA, MD
A Psychiatrist's Guide: Helping Parents Reach Their Depressed Tween
Paperback: $16.95
Kindle: $9.99

GAYANI DESILVA, MD
A Psychiatrist's Guide: Stop Teen Addiction Before It Starts
Paperback: $16.95
Kindle: $9.99
Audible: $14.95

JACK H. HARRIS
Father of the Blob: The Making of a Monster Smash and Other Hollywood Tales
Paperback: $16.95
Kindle/Nook: $9.99

New York Times Best Seller
CHRISTY WHITMAN
The Art of Having It All: A Woman's Guide to Unlimited Abundance
Paperback: $16.95
Kindle/Nook: $9.99
Audible Book: $13.00

Published by

TVGUESTPERT PUBLISHING

TVGuestpert Publishing
11664 National Blvd, #345
Los Angeles, CA. 90064
310-584-1504
www.TVGPublishing.com

TARA READE
Left Out: When The Truth Doesn't Fit In
Hardcover: $22.95
Kindle: $9.99

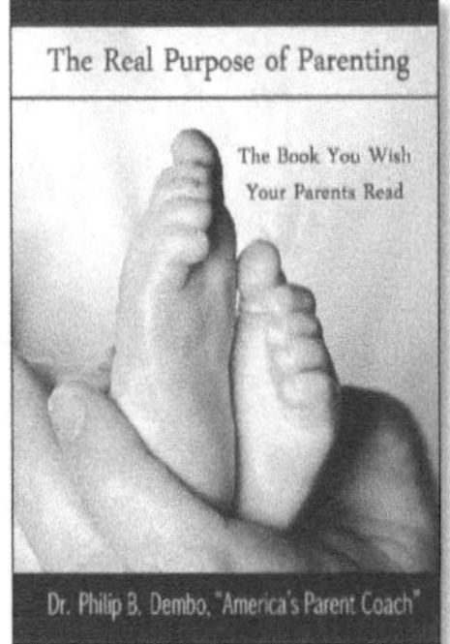

DR. PHILIP DEMBO
The Real Purpose of Parenting: The Book You Wish Your Parents Read
Paperback: $15.95
Kindle: $9.99
Audible: $23.95

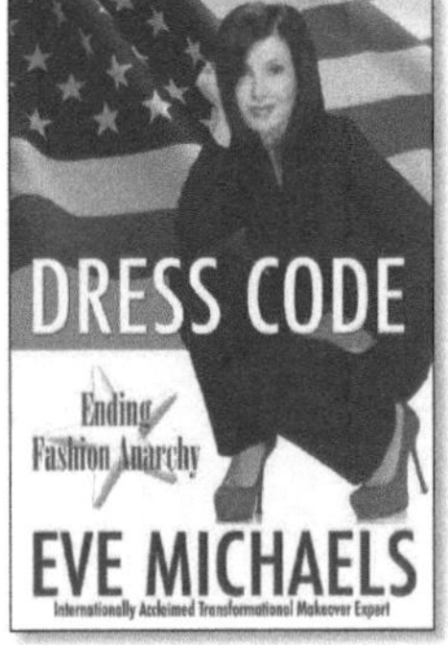

EVE MICHAELS
Dress Code: Ending Fashion Anarchy
Paperback: $15.95
Kindle/Nook: $9.99
Audible Book: $17.95